SWIMMING
SCIENTIFICALLY TAUGHT

FRANK EUGEN DALTON
FOUNDER OF THE DALTON SWIMMING SCHOOL

SWIMMING SCIENTIFICALLY TAUGHT

A PRACTICAL MANUAL FOR YOUNG AND OLD

By

FRANK EUGEN DALTON, P. S. A.

*Founder of the Dalton Swimming School, and
Originator of the Dalton Method*

EIGHTH EDITION—REVISED

With 89 Illustrations

FUNK & WAGNALLS COMPANY

NEW YORK AND LONDON

1931

TO MY FATHER

THE LATE CAPT. DAVIS DALTON

who swam the English Channel from Cape Gris Nez near Boulogne, France, to Sandgate, England, August 17-18, 1890; whose enthusiasm and unflagging interest in all matters pertaining to swimming and life-saving have been excelled by none, and who was a faithful practitioner of the methods herein set forth, this book is affectionately dedicated by his son,

THE AUTHOR

ACKNOWLEDGMENTS

To my brother, Mr. LOUIS C. DALTON, I am indebted for very valuable assistance in describing and picturing the various advanced strokes. To the AMERICAN RED CROSS I am grateful for permission to reproduce the text and pictures of the latest method of reviving persons apparently drowned; and to the NATIONAL COLLEGIATE ATHLETIC ASSOCIATION for its copyrighted version of the latest water-polo rules. To the Editor of *The Delineator* also I am indebted for permission to use, in part, the text and illustrations of a series of articles which I contributed to that magazine. For many of the pictures in the section on "Diving," showing the positions of the various dives, I owe a tribute of thanks to the AMERICAN SPORTS PUBLISHING COMPANY, which has kindly allowed me to make line drawings from illustrations in the volume of Spalding's Athletic Library entitled "The Science of Swimming."

ACKNOWLEDGMENT

I wish likewise to convey my thanks to Miss GERTRUDE KLEIN for her efficient help in posing for many of the new illustrations in this book, and to the ABRAMS PHOTO SERVICE for its skillful work in making the flashlight photographs from which these illustrations were reproduced. Finally, I must express my gratitude to Mr. EDWIN L. SHUMAN for his expert assistance in preparing the present edition for the press.

F. E. D.

CONTENTS

CONTENTS

CONTENTS

ILLUSTRATIONS

ILLUSTRATIONS

ILLUSTRATIONS

ILLUSTRATIONS

INTRODUCTION

WE live in an athletic age, and thousands of people count swimming among their favorite sports. Yet it is a surprizing fact that only one out of every twenty swims correctly. This small ratio of perfection, of course, is equally true of other sports; but it is doubly deplorable in swimming, because it is so easy to become proficient in that art. In golf and tennis we form bad habits of stance and swing which are difficult to overcome. With swimming the faults are not apt to be so deep-set. All the difference between right and wrong in swimming lies in certain comparatively simple problems of timing, and in a few refinements in the manner in which a stroke is executed.

One of the worst faults of the average swimmer is his or her inability to execute more than one or two strokes. A person knows the side stroke or the breast stroke, for example, and considers himself a competent swimmer, when in fact he is something of a danger to himself and a menace to others. Such a person usually can not swim far—the length of a pool, perhaps, or far enough to reach the diving raft at a beach. Something unusual occurs—a slightly stronger tide, one or another of the many surprizes constantly met with in the water—and this one-stroke, weak swimmer is drowned.

Hundreds of such people are drowned every summer. And the daily papers announce that "So-and-So, a good swimmer, was drowned yesterday while bathing at such-and-such a beach," while in reality he was not a good swimmer; in fact, all he had when he went into the water was a bathing suit and a large fund of misplaced confidence.

Often you see a person jump into the water and flounder about like a cross between a propeller and a windmill. If you were to suggest mildly that he did not know how to swim, you would arouse instant indignation. Yet actually such efforts in the water resemble swimming only as a fish's flopping about in a boat resembles walking. I have seen many a fish walk better than some "swimmers" swim. The subject reminds me of the man who asked his friend, "How do you spell Mississippi?" The friend answered: "M-I-S-I-S-I-P-P-I." "That's not correct," said the questioner. "I didn't say it was correct," answered the friend; "you asked me how *I* spelled it." A lot of people can show you how *they* swim—who can't swim at all.

We are none of us natural born swimmers. There are a few who seem to take to the water like fish, but the great majority are born with a dread of it—a dread handed down to them by their parents. I have an aunt who at one period had to make eight crossings yearly from London to Paris, and so great was her fear of the water that I have known her to wait twenty-four hours at Dover before deciding that the Channel was smooth enough for her to cross to Calais.

Then, again, many parents keep their children away from the water through fear that they will drown if they venture out of their depth. I would like to see swimming taught in all our public schools. Every new school building should be constructed with a swimming pool in the basement, and swimming lessons should be part of the curriculum, because child-hood is the best time for learning this admirable art. I start children from four years up.

Swimming gives better all-round develop-ment than any other sport. And it has so many branches and interesting phases: the various strokes, such as the side, back, breast, trudgen and crawl. Then the diving—fancy and trick diving. There are few finer sights than that of a clean-cut dive by either male or female. Next we have life-saving and re-suscitation: What more wonderful achieve-ment is there than being able to save a human being from drowning? Then for the experts we have water-polo, racing, and long distance swimming, which foster speed and endurance. Swimming-meets are helping to bring the sport to the fore, and every year it becomes more popular.

My father, Capt. DAVIS DALTON, who died August 6, 1899, was a great exponent of the back, breast, and side strokes. He had just the right build for a long-distance swimmer, being short—five feet seven inches—and broad, with powerful legs. He weighed 210 pounds. So great was his buoyancy in the water that he

CAPT. DAVIS DALTON
(Born in 1847, died in 1899)

The author's father, who in his day was the champion swimmer and lifesaver of the world, winning 148 medals of honor, and acquiring the unique record of having saved 278 lives.

could float with both arms held in the air, a very difficult feat, as the extra weight of the arms out of water usually forces the floater under the surface.

The most remarkable of Captain Dalton's long-distance swims were these, a majority of them being done entirely with the back stroke:

In December, 1889, he swam for twelve hours continuously at the Latchmere Public Baths, Battersea, London, England. On August 17-18, 1890, he swam the English Channel from Cape Gris Nez, France, to Sandgate, England, in two ebb-tides and two flood-tides, covering over sixty miles in 23 hours and 45 minutes—remarkable time when we consider the slowness of the back and breast strokes as compared with the present overarm, trudgen and crawl strokes. He swam most of the distance on his back, using the breast stroke only when the roughness of the water compelled it. He was blind for two weeks afterward from the effects of the salt water washing over his eyes. In July, 1891, Captain Dalton swam from Blackwall to Gravesend in the River Thames, about twenty miles in 6 hours and 35 minutes.

INTRODUCTION

In December of the same year he swam for sixteen hours continuously at the Dover Bath, England. In 1893 he gave exhibitions in the Fleischmann Pool at the Midway Plaisance, World's Columbian Exposition, Chicago.

My father was the chief organizer of the United States Volunteer Life-Saving Corps, and instructed many thousands of young Americans in the best and easiest methods of swimming, life-saving, and resuscitation. From his teachings I evolved the Dalton Method of instruction in swimming.

One object of the present treatise is to reduce the number of poor swimmers in the world, but my main object in writing it has been to help nervous and timid persons—those who think they can not learn to swim, because they have tried without attaining success. Many of these have had friends try to teach them—often by ducking them, which is a friend's first thought —and have gained nothing but a worse fear of the water. Children who cry and scream when first taken into the water should be handled very gently and never ducked.

To all those who have an unnatural fear of

INTRODUCTION

the water I offer this book in the hope that, by following its directions and persistently practising them, they will develop into safe and sane swimmers and divers.

F. E. D.

I

FIRST PRINCIPLES

I

FIRST PRINCIPLES

THE IMPORTANCE OF SWIMMING

THAT all persons ought to know how to safeguard themselves when in deep water is becoming more and more recognized. While swimming is one of the oldest pastimes known to man, and has had, and still has, its votaries in every country, civilized or uncivilized, it is curious that this most useful art should have been so neglected.

When an adult person is unable to swim, the fact points to something like criminal negligence on the part of someone. Every man, woman and child should learn how to do so. A person who can not swim is not only incurring needless danger himself, but in case of accident is liable to endanger the lives of those who happen to be near him. At as early an age as four children may be taught the art; none are too young, none too old to learn. Doctors recommend swimming as the best all-round exercise. It is especially beneficial to nervous people. Swimming reduces corpulence, improves the figure, expands the lungs, improves the circulation of the blood, builds up general health, increases vitality, gives self-confidence in case of danger, and exercises all the muscles in the body at one time. As an aid to the development of the muscular system, it excels other sports.

In other important ways it is a useful, and even a necessary accomplishment; no one knows when he may be called upon for a practical test of its merits. Yet only a small proportion of the entire population of the United States knows how to swim. A visit to any of the beaches along the Atlantic coast will convince one of this fact. There is no excuse for this ignorance, especially in a city like New York, with miles of water front and fine beaches at its very door; nor is there excuse in other places where ocean, lakes or rivers afford opportunities for swimming.

Swimming is a tonic alike for muscle and brain. The smallest child and the weakest woman can enjoy it equally with the strongest man. When slaves of the desk and of indoor occupations look forward to an all-too-brief vacation and seek the mountains or seashore to store up energy for another year's work, they should know how to swim. Poor, indeed, is the region which can not boast of a piece of water in which to take an invigorating plunge.

The importance of being able to swim was very generally recognized in ancient times, notably by the Romans. Roman youth, as early as the Republican era, when trained to bear arms, were made to include in their exercises bathing and swimming in the Tiber, where competitions were frequent. Cassius in his youth became renowned as a swimmer. Shakespeare, in a familiar passage, describes a race between him and Julius Cæsar, Cassius being made the speaker:

"I was born free as Cæsar; so were you:
We both have fed as well, and we can both
Endure the winter's cold as well as he.
For once, upon a raw and gusty day,
The troubled Tiber chafing with her shores,
Cæsar said to me, 'Dar'st thou, Cassius, now
Leap in with me into this angry flood
And swim to yonder point?' Upon the word,

SWIMMING SCIENTIFICALLY TAUGHT

Accoutred as I was, I plunged in,
And bade him follow; so, indeed he did.
The torrent roar'd; and we did buffet it
With lusty sinews, throwing it aside
And stemming it with hearts of controversy;
But ere we could arrive the point propos'd,
Cæsar cried, 'Help me, Cassius, or I sink.'
I, as Æneas, our great ancestor,
Did from the flames of Troy upon his shoulder
The old Anchises bear, so from the waves of Tiber
Did I the tired Cæsar.   And this man
Is now become a god."

Macaulay, in one of his "Lays of Ancient Rome," describes the scene which followed after Horatius had been left alone to face the troops of Lars Porsena, his codefenders having escaped across the bridge:

"Never, I ween, did swimmer,
In such an evil case,
Struggle through such a raging flood
Safe to the landing place:
But his limbs were borne up bravely,
By the brave heart within,
And our good father Tiber
Bare bravely up his chin."

Swimming has come to be regarded today as an indispensable adjunct to the education of the young. In many parts of Europe it has been admitted to the regular school curriculum. Of such paramount importance is it there held to be, that, on entering the army, the first thing taught a young recruit is swimming. On this side of the Atlantic its importance is daily becoming more evident. That the benefits to be derived from it have manifested themselves to municipalities is evidenced by the fact that, in addition to the opening of free swimming-baths on the water front of New York in summer, there have been established several indoor swimming-pools which are open and accessible the year around.

Swimming, aside from its importance as a possible means of self-preservation in case of shipwreck, the upsetting of pleasure-boats, or any of the accidents that so frequently happen on the water, or on occasion, as a means of saving life, is not only one of the best physical exercises known, but when one swims for exercise is also a medium through which one becomes conscious of receiving great pleasure. Almost any other form of exercise, after it has been participated in for some time, is apt to become something of an effort, or even a hardship. Swimming, on the other hand, continues to be exhilarating.

Unfortunately, those who have been best able to teach the art of swimming, through having the technical knowledge necessary to do so, and the proficiency, have not made systematic attempts to disseminate this knowledge by scientific methods. In this respect the author of this book has sought to improve upon the work of other instructors. He has endeavored to treat the subject scientifically and to use simple and concise language. His success as a teacher is attested by thousands of pupils who have acquired the principles of a system long known as the Dalton Method.

LEARNING BY THE BOOK

The question is often asked whether it is possible to learn to swim by studying a book or a series of articles. Much depends on the pupil. In the case of a very nervous person, it is improbable that this may be satisfactorily accomplished; it is almost absolutely necessary for such a pupil to have an instructor at the start, in order to overcome his or her dread of the water.

Where such dread or nervousness does not exist in any marked degree, study of a work such as this may be of unlimited advantage. By carefully following the instructions here laid down, it will be possible to become a very fair swimmer without the aid of an instructor or of any second person.

Naturally, it is not claimed that a majority of such self-taught swimmers will ever become experts, altho a few may do even this with the aid of the book alone; but there is a moral certainty that, with the exception of the afore-mentioned nervous beginners, anybody can gain a fair knowledge of the art of swimming in this manner. Numbers of very good swimmers have had no other tuition than that which came from the study of a book. Especially is this true when the beginner has followed the directions outlined in this book in the matter, first, of practising keeping the eyes and mouth open under water, which will eliminate all nervousness; and, second, of practising—out of the water—the movements used in the breast, side and back strokes, which are of inestimable aid when actually taking to the water.

Of course, where the swimmer desires to attain exact scientific knowledge of the art, it is almost absolutely necessary to have the aid of an instructor, who can watch for and correct any faults noticeable; because bad habits, once contracted, are difficult to eliminate later on.

If the lessons herein set forth are carefully applied, there is no reason why, with the exceptions mentioned, one should not become a good swimmer. This book contains a full exposition of all the methods that I have used in the last thirty years as a successful teacher of swimming.

GETTING USED TO THE WATER

One of the first things that I insist upon, with all the pupils of my three schools, is that they shall do plenty of under-water leg-kick practise. This is to accustom them to lying face down on the water. I start by having them stand with their backs to the side of the pool, at the shallow end, with the sole of the right foot against the side wall, the arms stretched out in front on top of the water, and the face tucked down between the arms.

Then, keeping the face and hands under water, the pupil pushes off with the right leg, pushing and straightening both arms and

(3) POSITION FOR PUSHING ACROSS UNDER WATER

legs. The impetus of the push should carry the body across the average width of a pool, which varies from twenty to thirty feet. If the tyro does not get across, the fault lies in the force of the push-off, and in not keeping the face under water. But several attempts will convince the most nervous beginner that the water will support his body, if he will only allow himself to lie on the water face down. When confidence is gained, the breast-stroke leg-kick can be practised. Even with a poor push-off, a couple of leg-kicks will drive the floater across the pool.

An added help is to keep the eyes open under water. Most beginners keep their eyes tightly closed all the time, mainly from fear. In my schools I get the pupils first to open their eyes both on and under water. It helps them to get used to being under water, and they lose their fear much more quickly. Another aid is teaching them to open their mouths under water. This can be practised at home in a wash-basin, or in a pail of water on a stool (Fig. 4). Go under with the mouth wide open. As long as you don't breathe in, the water can not force itself into your mouth and throat. All you have to do is to hold your breath. People get water into their lungs only when they breathe it in.

As soon as pupils find they can open their eyes and mouths and keep them open under water, it gives them confidence—takes away that instinctive dread of being under water.

FIRST PRINCIPLES

Then they don't mind lying on the water, practising the various strokes. My readers will find

(4) LEARNING TO GO UNDER WATER

this under-water work of real assistance as the
first logical step in learning to swim.

II

VARIOUS KINDS OF STROKES

II

VARIOUS KINDS OF STROKES

THE BACK STROKE

IT may seem odd to the beginner—and to a great many proficient swimmers, for that matter—that in teaching swimming by the Dalton system, I always begin by having pupils swim first on the back. Most instructors do just the reverse; but during thirty years of successful teaching, the proficiency of the graduated pupil has justified the method. There are a number of very good reasons why learners should begin by first swimming on the back. More especially is this true of nervous or timid pupils.

In the first place, the body floats more naturally and easily on the back. The crawl stroke, which is the first one taught by some instructors, requires the swimmer to hold the head under water, and the arms and legs do not coordinate as in the back and side strokes.

[43]

SWIMMING SCIENTIFICALLY TAUGHT

For that reason I always say that teaching the crawl stroke first to a beginner, especially a timid one, is like teaching a child to run before it can walk. In swimming on the back, the head rests on the water and needs no support from any other member of the body. At the same time the face is up and away from the water, so that the beginner encounters no difficulty in breathing, and there is no danger of the water entering the mouth—except when the swimmer throws water into the mouth on the first movement of the back stroke, through bringing the hands out of the water. So the moral is, always keep the hands under water. It is easier to do so, and there is not the added weight of the hands to be supported out of water.

Then, again, while on his back, as his face is turned upward, the beginner, especially if he is nervous, gains confidence from the very fact that he is not constantly looking into the water. And also, in contradistinction to all other strokes in swimming, the arms and legs move simultaneously—both arms and legs performing practically the same movements at the same time.

Thus the pupil, realizing the comparative

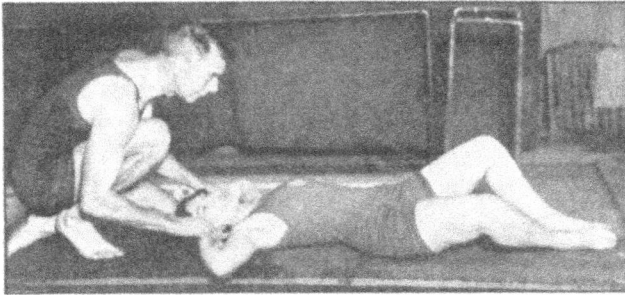

(5) BACK STROKE—FIRST ARM MOVEMENT

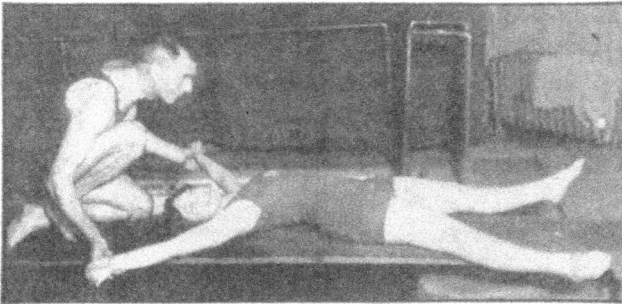

(6) BACK STROKE—SECOND ARM MOVEMENT

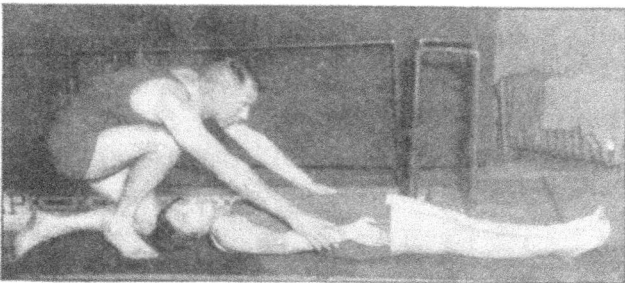

(7) BACK STROKE—THIRD ARM MOVEMENT

[45]

ease with which he has mastered this stroke, is imbued with such confidence that it becomes simply a matter of time and practise to acquire all other forms of swimming that he may wish to learn.

The first thing I do with a beginner, after he or she has donned a bathing suit (a suit in one piece is preferable, as it will not interfere with breathing) is to get the pupil to lie on the back, at full length on the marble, with the heels together, the toes out, the hands at the side of the body. Placing myself back of the pupil's head, the hands are drawn, with the fingers bent, up along the body till they touch the shoulders (Fig. 5), the elbows being well turned out. Then the arms are straightened out horizontally from the shoulder, the palms of the hands down (Fig. 6). Then the arms, being rigid, are brought down sharply to the side of the body (Fig. 7). These movements should be repeated several times until the pupil gets accustomed to them. When the movements become familiar, the hands can be brought farther back, above the level of the head. This gives a longer stroke for the third movement, which is the propelling part of the stroke.

(8) BACK STROKE—FIRST LEG MOVEMENT

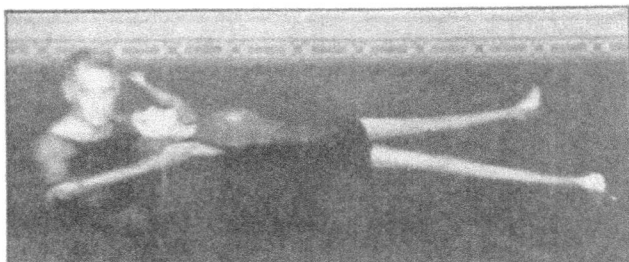

(9) BACK STROKE—SECOND LEG MOVEMENT

(10) BACK STROKE—THIRD LEG MOVEMENT

[47]

SWIMMING SCIENTIFICALLY TAUGHT

Next the leg movements are shown. The
heels are drawn up toward the body as far as
possible, with the knees well turned out (Fig.
8) ; the pupil then spreads the legs apart as far
as possible, the toes being pointed out straight
(Fig. 9). Next the pupil brings the legs
sharply together until the heels touch, the toes
being turned out (Fig. 10). After these movements have been repeated several times the
pupil can try the arm and leg movements together. The arms and legs are drawn up together as in Figs. 5 and 8, then the pupil
straightens out the arms and legs, as in Figs.
6 and 9, finishing the stroke by bringing the
arms and legs sharply together, as in Figs. 7
and 10.

When these movements have been mastered,
I take the pupil into the water. Letting his
head rest on my left shoulder, I take hold of the
pupil's right hand with my right hand, and go
with him through the three arm movements.
After practise I move over, resting the pupil's
head on my right shoulder and using my left
hand to guide the pupil's left hand through the
movements described above. When these are
well drilled in, I have the pupil hold on to bars

at the end of the pool and go through the three leg movements alone. This holding on to the bars gives the beginner courage to practise; he does not hold the body so tense as when lying on the water without support. I have always found it much better to get the arm and leg movements well drilled separately, so that they

(11) GETTING THE FACE UNDER WATER

become automatic, before trying the movements together.

To teach pupils how to regain their feet, I show them how to bend forward from the waist until the face is under water (Fig. 11); then they find the feet slowly sinking, and when the toes touch the bottom, the head can be raised out of the water.

Keep the arms in a straight line with the shoulders, palms facing down. This helps balance the body. Many stout people find trouble in bending from the waist and getting the face under water. To help these, I advise putting the chin on the chest and forcing the forehead under water. Keep bending from the waist— double up, as it were; keep bending and doubling until the head is under water (Fig. 11). As soon as the face is under water the feet will begin to sink; keep the face down until the feet touch bottom, then slowly stand up, keeping hands and arms spread on top of the water; otherwise if one arm is dropped the body will roll to one side. This standing up from back and floating position, as shown in the illustrations, imbues a beginner with confidence. And this reminds me of a recent occurrence. Swimming with my family at Sea Cliff, Long Island, I heard frantic cries of "Help! Help!" I swam toward the cries and discovered a very stout lady floating. "What's the matter?" I asked. "Help! Help! I'm floating." After I had put her on her feet, she told me she had never learned how to get on her feet from the floating position. She had always depended on friends to stand her up.

To accustom pupils to the water I teach them

to open the eyes and mouth under water. This is much simpler than non-swimmers imagine. Care must be taken not to open the eyes too wide. At the first few attempts the pupil will feel amazed, on opening the eyes, at the distance of the vision under water.

To find out if the pupil's eyes are open, I hold my hand out under water and extend two, three or four fingers. If the eyes have been opened, the· pupil will tell me the correct number. Then, to find out if the mouth is open, I place a finger between the teeth. When the eyes and mouth have been opened separately, I teach my pupils to open eyes and mouth together. Learning to open the mouth under water is very simple when the beginner once realizes that the water cannot force itself down his throat unless it is breathed in. The only thing is not to breathe in, just hold the breath. Good outside practise in this trick may be had by holding a watch in your hand, taking a deep breath, closing your mouth, and seeing how long you can hold your breath without breathing through the nose. This practise will improve your capacity of holding your breath, which is a great help in swimming and diving.

[51]

It is wonderful how much confidence the novice gains on realizing his ability to open the eyes and keep the mouth open under water.

A life-preserver tied around the waist makes it unnecessary for the instructor to hold the pupil, so that he can better direct the movements. Thus the pupil, being held up by a preserver, makes headway, care being taken to do the movements slowly and together.

Now, to combine the arm and leg movements:

One—Draw the hands up to the top of the shoulders, elbows turned out and legs up, knees and toes well turned out.

Two—Arms out in a straight line with shoulders, and legs spread as far apart as possible, toes pointed.

Three—Bring the straightened-out arms and legs sharply together, and breathe.

These movements should be practised with a count of one, two, three, breathe—one, two, three, breathe. I advise twenty-five times first with the arms, then the same with the legs, and then twenty-five times together. By this method the beginner not only learns correct movements and breathing, but also benefits greatly from the exercise which these entail. At each lesson I let a little of the air out of the preserver which supports the beginner in the water; and at the end of the fourth, or at latest the fifth lesson, the pupil swims without a preserver.

Then the pupil is shown how to turn around. The knees should be drawn up, as in Fig. 8;

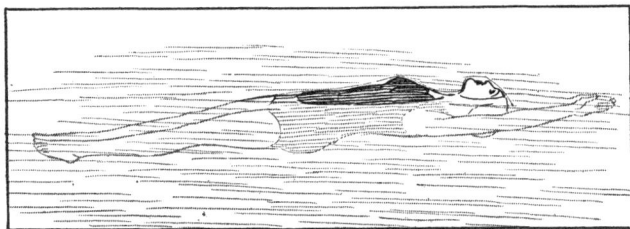

(12) BACK PLUNGING

then, to turn to the left, the right arm movements alone should be used, holding the left arm in a straight line with the shoulder; then continue to use the three arm movements with the right arm, until you have turned completely around in the water. To turn the other way, use the other arm.

Next the pupil is shown how to float. The legs are straight, toes pointed, and the arms

[53]

extended back beyond the head, as in Fig.
12; the hands, about six inches apart, are kept
under water. Deep breaths should be drawn
through the mouth and forced into the lungs.
The pupil will notice that, at each inflation of
the lungs, the body rises in the water, and sinks
correspondingly when the air is expelled. This
practise shows how buoyant the body is. The
more limp one lies, the more buoyant the body
becomes.

Since I started the Dalton Swimming School
in 1900, at 19 West 44th Street, New York
City, later taking my brother, Louis C. Dalton,
as partner, I have always shown my method of
teaching swimming scientifically, which is ex-
actly the reverse of the methods of other instructors; that is, teaching pupils how to swim
on their backs first, before teaching them other
strokes. Another innovation of mine is the use
of the Dalton nose-clip, a clip that pinches the
nostrils tightly together, keeping the water out
of the nose and forcing the pupil to breathe
through the mouth, which is the correct way
of breathing while swimming. The more air
one gets into the lungs the lighter one is in the
water, making swimming easier. The reason

so many would-be swimmers get winded very quickly is simply that they try to breathe through the nose. The main thing about breathing in all the strokes is to keep the mouth open all the time. With the mouth open, air can come in and out of its own accord and the pupil does not have to worry about the breathing.

Many people suffer with sinus trouble, and this is aggravated when water is inhaled through the nose. The result is so unpleasant, and is so liable to be followed by headache, that it often produces an utter distaste for continuing in the water. This can not happen when one of my nose-clips is used; besides, the nose-clip teaches the right way of breathing—it makes a mouth-breather out of a swimmer. The air can be taken in more quickly and in larger quantities through the mouth. Try it yourself in a basin or pail of water, as in Fig. 4. Note how unpleasant it is when the water enters the nose; it irritates the membrane. Now try again, only pinch the nostrils tightly together with the first finger and thumb. The difference will be noted at once. I am sure, from observation, that if the majority of begin-

[55]

ners and non-swimmers would use nose-clips, swimming and diving would become popular sports with the masses. In former years a woman's chief objection to going swimming was the trouble of drying long hair. With bobbed hair, cotton in the ears, and a nose-clip, being on and under water leaves no unpleasant results.

THE DALTON STROKE

Many elderly people who take up swimming find difficulty in spreading the legs for the back and breast strokes. Noticing this, it occurred to me that I could invent a method which would make it easier for beginners who do not swim on their initial attempts and who can not spread their legs for the regular kick. So I devised a stroke of my own for the benefit of nervous, timid, or elderly women, and found it so successful that I now teach it to all my pupils. Instead of going head first, as in the back stroke, one moves feet first through the water. To show the stroke, I describe three stages, which should be practised out of the water on a bench, as in the illustrations.

VARIOUS KINDS OF STROKES

Hold the legs perfectly straight, then drop the right leg in the water (Fig. 13); straighten right leg again, at the same time dropping the left leg perpendicularly from the knee down. Continue this movement, up and down from the knee, kicking the water behind you from the

(13) BEGINNING THE DALTON STROKE

back of calf and heel; this propels you forward, if you bring the leg up easily and down with force.

Start with the arms straight at sides of body, palms facing out, fingers cupped; bring straightened-out arms around in line with the shoulders, fingers still being cupped; draw arms

[57]

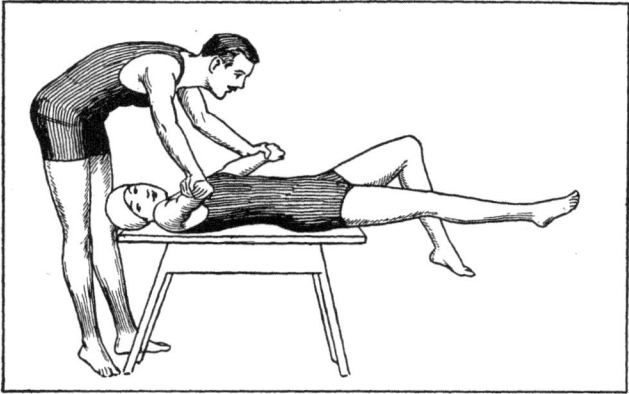

(14) THE DALTON STROKE—SECOND PHASE

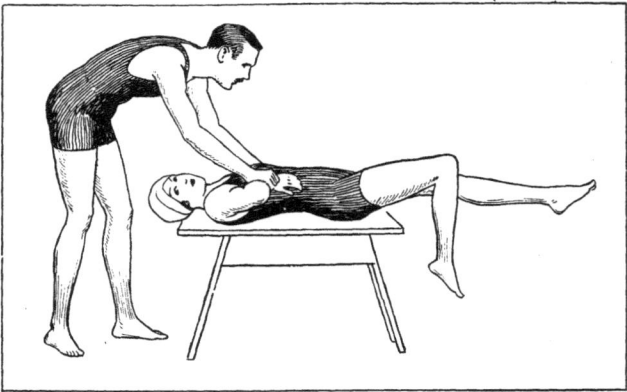

(15) THE DALTON STROKE—JUST BEFORE FINISHING

in to armpits, as in Fig. 15, hands being still cupped. Finish movement by bringing hands down to sides of body. The arm and leg movements combined are awkward in the first few attempts, as the movements do not work in unison; but practise out of the water (Figs. 14 and 15) will certainly facilitate matters when you undertake the movement in the water.

When teaching this stroke I always stand back of the pupil, supporting the body by holding one hand between the shoulder-blades and using the other hand to help one of the arm movements, changing hands to accustom both the pupil's arms to this circular movement. Hands should be kept about two inches under the surface of the water all the time, otherwise the water is thrown over the face every time the hands come out of the water.

To combine the arm and leg movements: Drop right leg from knee; keep left leg straight on water, hands to side of body, palms turned out, fingers cupped. Raise right leg; drop left leg from knee; bring hands around in line with shoulders, as in Fig. 14. Raise left leg and drop right leg; bring arms in to armpits as in Fig. 15; raise right leg and drop left leg; bring

[59]

hands down to sides of body. Continue with
a count—one, two, three.

To improve still further the arm movements
of this stroke: instead of stopping when the
straightened-out arms come in line with the
shoulders, continue with the arms still under
the surface until the backs of the hands touch,

(16) EXTENDED ARM MOVEMENT FOR DALTON STROKE

as in Fig. 16; pause here a second and breathe.
Then slowly bend elbows out and drop hands
under water until finger-tips touch shoulders;
gently slide palms of hands over shoulders and
continue along side of body until hands reach
starting position again. This is a very easy
and graceful movement. Care must be taken
to keep the hands under water as much as possible. To keep in time with leg movements,

make it a one, two, three, four count for arms; one, two with arms until back of hands touch, as in Fig. 16; three, hands on shoulders, and four when hands get to side of body at finish of movement.

THE BACK AND DALTON STROKE

In teaching this stroke I revise both the back and the Dalton stroke with the life-preserver on. After the pupil has covered a distance with the back stroke, instead of making a turn to retrace, I show him how to revert to the Dalton stroke, thus avoiding the necessity of turning around. When changing from the back stroke to the Dalton stroke the legs should be brought together and the hands put straight to the sides of the body; then either stroke can be continued. The next move is to let a little air out of the life-preserver. The pupil then begins again on the same strokes. After several trips up and down the pool, more air is let out, with more trips up and down the pool, and so on until there is no air left in the preserver.

So slight will be the difference that the pupil

will hardly notice it. As long as the back is well hollowed, the upper part of the body will float; but directly the body is doubled up, the head and feet begin to sink, so that the teacher must follow close to make the pupil keep the back well hollowed and the chest expanded. Beginners will be surprized at the ease with which back strokes propel the body through the water without any undue effort. To one who has never been used to swimming without support it gives a wonderful feeling of exhilaration to propel one's self through the water and then, when tired, to bring the arms slowly back under water until the thumbs come together behind the head and the knees are drawn up to the floating position, while one inhales deep breaths through the mouth, thereby sustaining the body well up in the water.

THE SIDE STROKES

The side stroke is used for long distance swimming and is easy to learn on either side. The pupil should count the movements and be deliberate while doing the strokes. Splashing

VARIOUS KINDS OF STROKES

and fast strokes always denote an indifferent swimmer. Easy and graceful swimming can be acquired only by taking slow strokes and keeping the hands under the surface, thereby obviating all tendency to push the arms through the air instead of the water. While practising these movements the head must be kept well

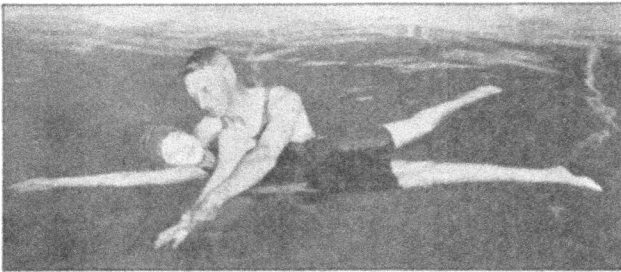

(17) POSITION 2, RIGHT SIDE STROKE

down so as to be supported by the water and the right arm held straight ahead as in Figure 17 until the left arm and leg movements are mastered.

RIGHT SIDE—Practise these movements on the floor:

Arm Strokes: Extend the right arm until it straightens in front, keeping it in this position,

[63]

(18) RIGHT SIDE STROKE—FIRST ARM AND LEG MOVEMENTS

(19) SECOND ARM AND LEG MOVEMENTS

(20) THIRD ARM AND LEG MOVEMENTS

thus making it easier to acquire balance. (Fig. 17.) Place the left hand at the left side. Movement I—Draw the left arm slowly up to the chest, palm out (Fig. 18). Movement II— Extend the left arm as far forward as possible (Fig. 19). Movement III—Draw the left arm down to the side of the upper (left) leg, being careful not to bend the elbow (Fig. 20).

Leg Strokes: Movement I—Bend both legs back together from the knees down, or right instep on left knee. Movement II—Extend the left leg backward from the hip as far as possible, and the right leg forward from the hip as far as possible (Fig. 19). Movement III— Snap the legs, which should then be perfectly straight, together (Fig. 20). Now combine both Movements I, as in Fig. 18, then both Movements II, as in Fig. 19, and both Movements III, as in Fig. 20. After the pupil is more advanced he may use his right arm by extending it out from and bringing it back to the right side of the body, on counts one and three.

Breathing: Inhale as the left arm is swept alongside the body. Exhale when the left arm is extended forward.

[65]

(21) LEFT SIDE STROKE—FIRST ARM AND LEG MOVEMENTS

(22) LEFT SIDE STROKE—SECOND ARM AND LEG
MOVEMENTS

(23) LEFT SIDE STROKE—THIRD ARM AND LEG MOVEMENTS

[66]

VARIOUS KINDS OF STROKES

LEFT SIDE—The same procedure as for the right side may be followed lying on the left side. This is important to learn, as the pupil should swim equally well on either side. It will also help him to acquire good form.

Arm Strokes: Movement I—Draw the right arm forward close to the chest, palm out, elbow at the side (Fig. 21). Movement II—Extend the right arm forward as far as possible, keeping the hand about six inches below the surface (Fig. 22). Movement III—Sweep the right arm sharply down to the right side, then rest (Fig. 23). The left arm is not used, but is held straight in front to help balance the body. When the pupil is proficient the left arm may be extended and brought back as on the right side.

Leg Strokes: Movement I—Bend both legs back, from the knees down, or left instep on right knee (Fig. 21). Movement II—Spread the legs as wide apart as possible, the right back from the hip and the left forward from the hip (Fig. 22). Movement III—Snap the straightened-out legs together (Fig. 23).

Combine the Arm Movements with the Leg Movements: Movement I—Draw the right

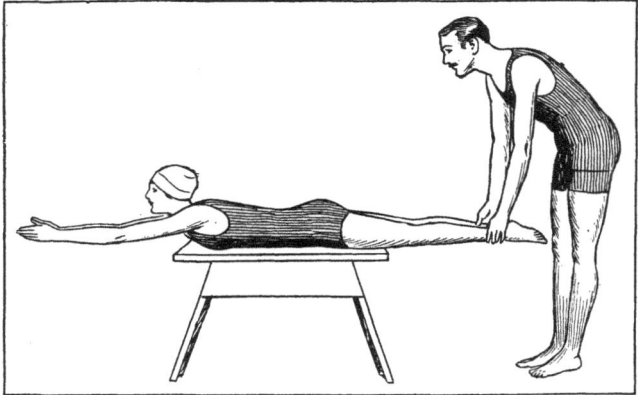

(24) BREAST STROKE—READY TO BEGIN

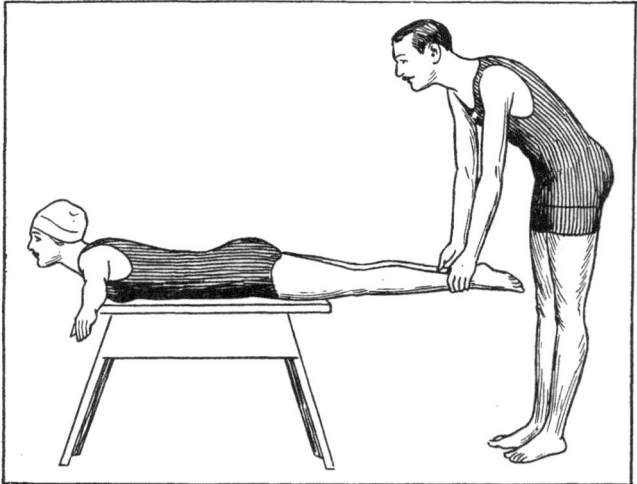

(25) BREAST STROKE—FIRST ARM MOVEMENT

[68]

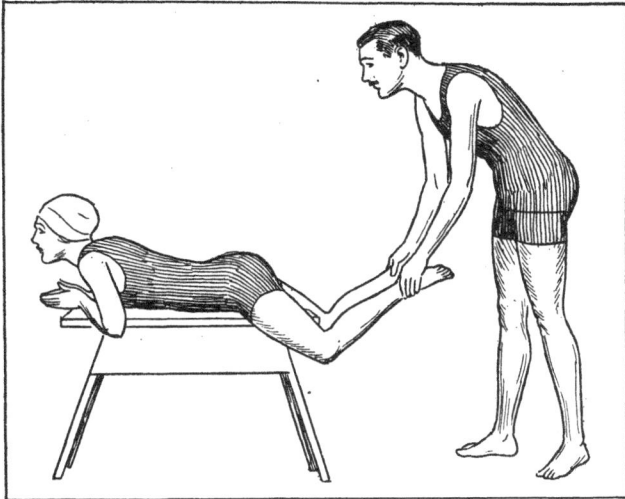

(26) BREAST STROKE—SECOND MOVEMENT

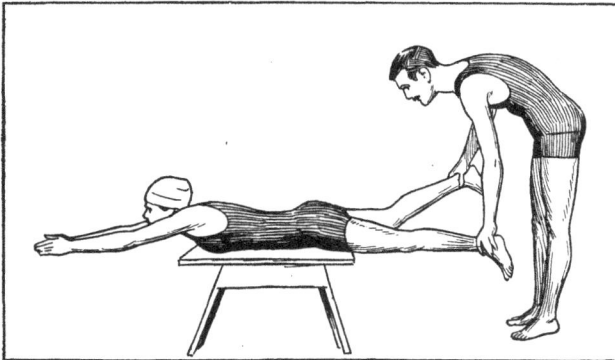

(27) BREAST STROKE—THIRD MOVEMENT

arm close to the chest, palm out; bend both legs back, from the knees down (Fig. 21). Movement II—Extend the right arm forward and spread the legs wide apart (Fig. 22). Movement III—Sweep the right arm down to right side and snap the legs together, then rest while your body is being propelled through the water (Fig. 23). Hold the head so that the mouth is above the surface, and breathe as on the right side.

THE BREAST STROKE

The breast stroke in swimming has been handed down from earliest times. It is usually the first stroke taught beginners by instructors, but I have found from many years' experience that better and quicker results may be obtained by starting the pupil with the back and Dalton strokes. The breast stroke is more difficult because the head has to be supported above water.

Any part of the body when held out of the water is dead weight, and as the head is all bone, muscle and brain, it is the heaviest part. That is why, using the breast stroke, it is much harder to keep the mouth and nostrils above

VARIOUS KINDS OF STROKES

water. The breast stroke is so universally identified with swimming that every beginner wants to learn it. It is only on this account that I teach it.

When learning to swim in a pool, the best method is to learn how to do the strokes under water, with head submerged. The reason for this is, that the beginner can concentrate on the strokes without having to worry about keeping the face above water for breathing. After the strokes are done fairly well together, the pupil can be supported on the surface of the water with a life-preserver or well-inflated bladder.

First we will begin to practise the movements on dry land as shown in the illustrations. Start by lying flat on the stomach, palms together, arms straight in front, legs straightened out, heels together, and toes turned out (Fig. 24).

Arm Strokes: Movement I—Turn palms of hands until they face down. Bring the straightened-out arms around in line with the shoulders (Fig. 25).

Movement II—Bring palms of the hands together by dropping the elbows (Fig. 26), taking care to keep the hands on the same level right through the three movements.

Movement III—Shoot the arms straight in front to the starting position, palms together again (Fig. 27).

When these movements are fixed in the mind, try the leg strokes.

Leg Strokes: Movement I—Bring the heels up toward the body, heels together with toes and knees well turned out as in Illustration 26.

Movement II—Shoot the legs as far as possible with toes turned out (Fig. 27).

Movement III—Continue by bringing the straightened-out legs sharply together with a snap until heels touch again as in Figures 24 and 25.

Now try the leg and arm movements together.

Movement I—Turn the hands, palms down, and bring the straightened-out arms around in line with shoulders. Use the arms alone, the legs being kept still (Fig. 25).

Movement II—Bring the hands together by dropping the elbows and keeping the hands near the surface of the water, at same time drawing the legs up to the body (Fig. 26), knees and toes well turned out.

Movement III—Shoot the arms out straight

to the starting position. At the same time kick the legs as far as possible (Figs. 27 and 24) and bring straightened-out legs together with a snap, counting, one, two—legs alone. To make it easier for my pupils to learn these movements, I have them count, one two, three, four. The count goes, one, two, legs together; three, arms alone; four, together, which means the arms stay still on two count and legs still on three count.

After practise, one will get the rhythm, so that the movements will be automatic. When this point is reached, try the stroke in the water, practising at a depth of not more than four feet.

Start by lying in the water face down, with arms straight in front, and trying the leg movement first. Draw the legs up to the body, then put all the force in the out *wide* and sharply *together* kick. After this comes the three—arms alone—wait, draw the legs up again for four count. A good idea is to keep the eyes open under water and count mentally. After the complete leg-kick, bend back until the feet touch the bottom of the pool. This exercise will also improve the wind when the legs begin to work naturally.

Attempt the arm movements alone, head under water. Start by floating on water face down. Bring straightened-out arms in front in line with shoulders to count of three, arms alone. Next bring the hands together to the chest, dropping elbows to the count of four, together. Shoot arms out straight in front, palms together to count of one, two. This is the most important part of the arm strokes, because the arms are cutting a way through the water, while the double leg-kick is driving the body ahead. When the arm movements are being done fairly well, try the arm and leg movements together with head under water. Start with arms straight in front, hands together and legs straightened out behind, heels touching; toes and knees well turned out (Fig. 24).

Movement I—Bring arms around in line with shoulders. Legs should be kept still to count of three, arms alone, as in Fig. 25.

Movement II—Draw arms in till the palms touch by dropping elbows. Bring the legs up toward the body, knees and toes well turned out, to count of four, together as in Fig. 26.

VARIOUS KINDS OF STROKES

Movement III—Shoot arms straight in front, palms together, and at the same time do a double movement with the legs. Shoot them out as wide as possible and bring them straight together till the heels touch, to count of one,

(28) TEACHING THE BREAST STROKE

two, legs together (Figs. 27 and 24). Then go back to the first movement. By studying the accompanying figures, the swimmer will more readily grasp the combined movements. After practise, these combined movements will become mechanical, and can be tried by raising the face just enough above the surface of the

[75]

water to allow the breath to be taken in. Naturally all beginners swim very low in the water at first, but as the stroke is improved the breathing becomes easier and the body will rise as confidence is gained.

(29) BREAST STROKE—COMBINING ARM-SWEEP AND LEG-KICK

When teaching this stroke, in the water, I support the pupil with my right arm around the waist, hold his left wrist with my left hand, and go through the arm and leg movements as shown in the illustrations (Figs. 28, 29 and 30). When the pupil is learning alone, I advise the

VARIOUS KINDS OF STROKES

use of a life preserver till the rhythm begins to assert itself; then he can discard the life preserver and practise the stroke with face under water, thus being able to think of his arm and leg movements without the exertion of holding his head above water.

(30) BREAST. STROKE—RETURNING TO FIRST POSITION BY BRINGING LEGS TOGETHER

To those who experience difficulty in getting their breath, I advise turning the head (not body) to the right, which brings the mouth out of the water far enough for the swimmer to breathe through the left or upper side of the mouth.

CHANGING FROM BREAST TO SIDE, BACK AND DALTON STROKES

The change from breast to side, back or Dalton stroke, or vice versa, is simple if done slowly. Let us assume that we are using the breast stroke and wish to turn to another stroke. When in the position of Fig. 30, we roll over on the right side, bringing left arm to side of body, keeping right arm straight ahead and legs together. We are now in the third position of the side stroke (Fig. 20).

Now, after doing a couple of side strokes, say we wish to change to the back stroke. After coming to the third position of the side stroke, we continue to bring the left arm over the body and turn the mouth up. The weight of the left arm and the turn of head will roll us over on our backs to the third position of the back stroke (Fig. 10).

Next we may change to the Dalton stroke. After doing a couple of back strokes and coming again to the third position, drop the right leg and turn palms of hands facing out as in Figs. 13 and 14, and continue in Dalton stroke.

VARIOUS KINDS OF STROKES

To reverse, straighten out both legs, toes pointed, turn palms of hands to side of body and continue on back stroke. To turn to right side, bring left arm and hand over body, straighten right arm ahead and bring left leg on right. This will roll one over to third position of side stroke (Fig. 20). To turn to breast stroke, put face under water, both arms straight ahead, and bring left leg over. Strokes can then be done under water. After that, with face raised for air, continue breast stroke.

For long distance swimming these turns are very necessary, and all beginners should practise them, thus becoming more at home in the water and better able to handle themselves on the various strokes.

III

STROKES FOR ADVANCED SWIMMERS

III

STROKES FOR ADVANCED SWIMMERS

SINGLE OVER-ARM STROKES

AFTER mastering the right and left side strokes, the pupil takes to this stroke very quickly, because in reality it is a combination of both.

RIGHT SINGLE OVER-ARM STROKE —*Arm Strokes:* Movement I—Lie on the right side, right arm drawn in toward the body, hand pointing forward, left arm resting at the left side of body, palm out. Movement II—Lift the left arm out of the water and extend forward, but at arm's length, away from the head, the right arm motionless. Movement III— Sweep the left arm sharply down to the side and extend the right arm straight ahead.

Leg Strokes: Movement I—Bend both legs back from the knees down, keeping the knees and ankles together. Movement II—Place the left leg back from the hip, and the right leg forward from the hip. Be sure the legs are perfectly straight. Movement III—Snap both straightened-out legs sharply together, then rest.

(31) RIGHT SINGLE OVER-ARM STROKE

Combine with the Arms: Lie on right side. Movement I—Hold the left arm down to the side, palm out, right arm drawn in toward the body, hand pointed forward, legs bent back from the knees down. Movement II—Lift the left arm out of the water, at the same time spreading the legs apart, keeping the right arm motionless (Fig. 31). Movement III—This

[84]

STROKES FOR ADVANCED SWIMMERS

movement must be done sharply. Draw the
left arm down to the side, extending the right
arm straight ahead, while snapping the legs
straight together as in Fig. 32.

LEFT SINGLE OVER-ARM STROKE—
Arm Strokes: Lie on left side. Movement I

(32) RIGHT SINGLE OVER-ARM STROKE—FINISH

—Place the right arm at right side of body,
palm out, the left arm held close to the side.
Movement II—Lift the right arm out of the
water, being careful to hold it as far away as
possible to avoid splashing, the left arm motionless. Movement III—Sweep the right arm
sharply down to the right side, and extend the
left arm straight ahead.

[85]

Leg Strokes: Movement I—Bend the legs back from the knees down, knees and ankles together. Movement II—Bring the right leg back from the hip, and extend the left forward from the hip. Movement III—Snap the straightened-out legs sharply together.

Combine the Arms and Legs: Movement I —Hold the right arm at full length to right side, palm out; the left hand should be held well in toward the body, pointing forward; bend both legs back from the knees down, knees and ankles together. Movement II—Lift the right arm out of the water and spread the legs apart; while doing this movement the left arm is motionless. Movement III—Bring the right arm sharply down to the right side, extending the left arm forward, and snapping the legs quickly together.

Breathing: Inhale through the mouth, at the moment when each arm is performing the downward stroke, as the mouth will then be clear of the water. Exhale immediately the arm is extended forward.

Almost everybody finds it easier to learn the right single over-arm stroke before the left, unless he is left handed.

STROKES FOR ADVANCED SWIMMERS

THE ENGLISH RACING STROKE

The English racing stroke (Fig. 33) is a great deal more difficult to learn than any of

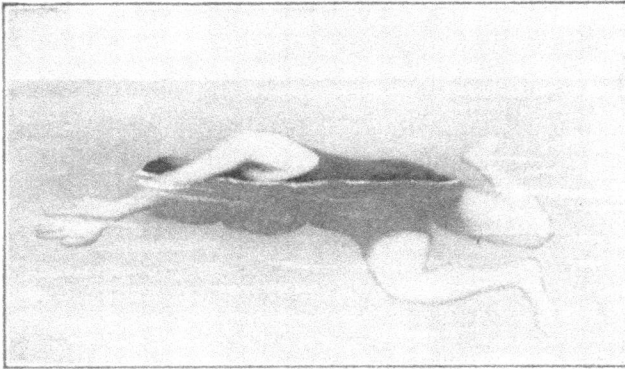

(33) THE ENGLISH RACING STROKE

the advanced strokes that we have reached so far, but once the student is proficient, it is one of the prettiest strokes.

The Arm Movements should first be learned. Lie on the right side (but, if the pupil prefers, it can be done equally well on the left). Hold the left arm at the left side. Then raise it out of the water, bending the elbow; the hand should enter palm out, and about six inches below the surface, then extended as far forward as possible. Next sweep the left arm down to the side sharply. Extend the right arm straight ahead, drawing it in toward the body with a semi-circular scoop.

The Leg Movements are very difficult, and a great deal of practise will be necessary before the pupil is ready to combine them with the arm movements. The legs are spread apart and snapped together as in the side stroke, but instead of stopping with this scissors kick, an extra small circle kick is required.

Breathing: Inhale by turning the head as the left arm is swept down to the left side; exhale under water when the left arm is extended forward. Pay great attention to breathing on each stroke, as this is a great deal more essential than acquiring speed, if you wish to swim any distance. Because of improper breathing with this stroke, people who can not swim very well complain more about getting winded quickly than they do about anything else.

STROKES FOR ADVANCED SWIMMERS

THE DOUBLE OVER-ARM STROKE

The double over-arm stroke, while difficult to master, will not prove so for the student who has learned the English racing stroke. Learn

(34) THE DOUBLE OVER-ARM STROKE

the double over-arm to acquire form. For racing the crawl will answer.

Arm Strokes: Place the left arm at the left side, then lift it out of the water, bending the elbow and stretching it as far forward as possible; now draw the hand down through the water so that it is swept to the side. The right

[89]

arm should be at the right side in position to come forward perfectly rigid at third movement of left arm. There must be enough roll of the body to allow the right arm to come out of the water to insure proper breathing. Sweep the right arm down through the water as the left arm is raised out of the water. Hold the face under the water, except when you inhale after the left arm has passed the mouth; exhale when under as the right arm comes forward.

Leg Strokes: The legs perform the regular scissors kick at the same time with left arm action, then they cross over and make a smaller scissors kick in conjunction with right arm action while the body is rolling, as in Fig. 34. The arms and legs should be relaxed, except when the arms are making their sweep and the legs are snapping together; otherwise the pupil will be under a constant strain, which is not conducive to good form in swimming. You may find it very difficult at the start to time this stroke.

STROKES FOR ADVANCED SWIMMERS

THE TRUDGEN STROKE

This was one of the racing strokes before the advent of the crawl, and was considered by some swimmers the fastest stroke. It is quite tiring and should be used only for short distances. A great many swimmers modify this stroke to suit themselves, but there is only one scientific way. The arms are held perfectly straight, and lifted well above the water on every stroke. First practise with the arms alone. Lie on right side with the right arm extended forward at full length, left arm perfectly straight at left side. Draw the right arm sharply down through the water to the right side, turning the body at the same time, lifting the left arm out of the water and extending it straight in front.

Position 1—The legs should be drawn up, heels together, knees spread as the right arm starts to come forward and the left arm starts to come down through the water (Fig. 35). Position 2—Spread the legs apart as the right arm continues to extend forward and the left arm continues to be pulled down through the water.

(35) TRUDGEN STROKE—FIRST POSITION

(35-a) TRUDGEN STROKE—SECOND POSITION

(35-b) TRUDGEN STROKE—THIRD POSITION

(36) TRUDGEN STROKE—FOURTH POSITION

Position 3—Snap the legs together as the left arm is swept below the surface to the left thigh, and the right arm is extended as far forward as

[93]

possible. These three leg movements must be done very quickly. Position 4—The left' arm is brought forward, then the right down to the side; the legs remain motionless (Fig. 36). For racing purposes, the arms may be bent at the elbows. The head rests on the water, the mouth just above the surface for breathing on Positions 2 and 3.

THE CRAWL AND TRUDGEN-CRAWL

The crawl and trudgen-crawl are by all means the fastest strokes for propelling the human body through the water up to date. The crawl stroke as originally introduced was a combination of the trudgen arm stroke with a leg drive used by the natives of the South Sea Islands. This stroke has since been changed by leading swimmers, so that it is probably entirely different now from what it was when originally introduced. A great many amateur and professional coaches advocate the teaching of the crawl to beginners. I would have the pupil note the difference between a coach and a swimming instructor. The coach's pupil knows how to swim, but the instructor must first teach his pupil. The coaches are so much in favor of the crawl that they advocate teaching it to everybody in the beginning. On the other hand, the instructor knows that it would take twice as long to teach the crawl to a nervous beginner.

Because of the attitude of the coaches, I have had a deluge of requests from novices that they be taught the crawl. I therefore wish to spread broadcast the fact that it is *absolutely essential* for pupils to acquire confidence by first learning the simple back, side, and Dalton strokes. The principal reason for this is the fact that 85 per cent. of all beginners are too nervous and timid to immerse their faces. As this stroke must be swum with the face under water, it will readily be seen why I differ with the coaches referred to. The crawl, like all other strokes in swimming, must be done slowly, and with the body relaxed, to attain speed.

Bend all your efforts to acquiring form; speed will come later with constant practise, patience and perseverance. The crawl may be done correctly with varying details, depending on the physique of the swimmer, and ability of the coach to apply the proper methods to his pupil. I have swum the crawl in all its various

(37) THE CRAWL STROKE

details, and will explain the method I have found fastest and easiest for the pupil (Fig. 37). The crawl and the trudgen-crawl are the strokes par excellence for racing purposes, as experience has demonstrated.

Leg Strokes: Extend the arms at full length in front of the head with face under water, while practising with the legs. While doing this hold the breath, but not after you have learned the completed stroke. When practising these movements you must kick the legs a trifle faster than will be necessary when combining with the arm movements.

The legs must be relaxed, especially at the hips, kicking them up and down alternately; in doing this do not open them more than from about ten to fifteen inches as in Fig. 38. This will depend a great deal on the physique and buoyancy of the swimmer. The toes should be pointed behind and the feet turned inward. Be careful that you do not make the mistake of kicking them too high or opening them too much, also that they do not come out of the water. You will readily know if you are making these mistakes, because the legs will become tired and cramped very quickly.

[97]

Some fast swimmers bend their legs at the knees as illustrated in Fig. 39; others take a sort of pedaling motion by bending the ankles back and forth. This is done by bringing the toes up as the leg rises, and pointing them down as the leg snaps back. At the present time the fastest sprinters swim without the great bend

(38) THE CRAWL STROKE—PROPER LEG POSITION

in the knee; some bend the knees slightly to help relax the legs.

The trudgen-crawl kick is a combination of the crawl and the trudgen, and the reason it is generally used in preference to the crawl is because it is less tiring, thus affording greater speed for long distances. This may be swum in either two, four, six, or eight beats. The eight-

STROKES FOR ADVANCED SWIMMERS

beat is not used very often. The six-beat is
used by most of the fastest swimmers, but the
four-beat is the easiest for pupils to learn and
time; it also is very speedy. The legs should be
kept close together at all times, and after taking
two, four, six or eight beats, whichever the case
may be, the kick should be so formed that the

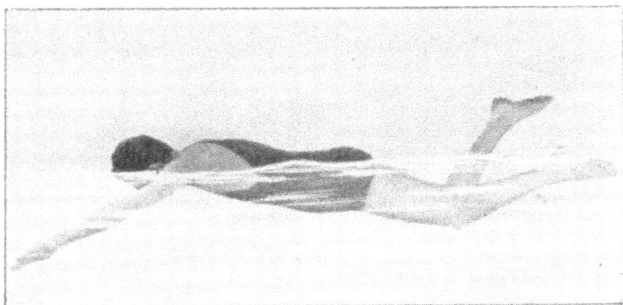

(39) THE CRAWL STROKE—EXTRA LEG WORK

first and fourth amount to narrow scissors
kicks; then follow with the regular thrash kick,
which is straight up and down, as illustrated in
Fig. 40. Point the legs and turn the feet in
slightly.

Mostly the trudgen-crawl kick is done on
six-beat time, the count going one, two, three
for the trudgen-scissors kick and four, five, six

for the crawl thrash.   This combination should
be diligently practised alone, without using the
arms, until it is mastered.   Some of the present-
day long-distance swimmers, both men and
women, use this combination kick.

Quite a few swimmers believe their legs are

(40) THE TRUDGEN-CRAWL KICK

of little assistance, but you will find, if you
practise the movements alone the way I suggest,
that the legs play a very prominent part in your
stroke.   You will be able to make good speed
without using the arms.

When these movements are thoroughly mastered, after trying all the different variations
to discover which suits your particular need,

you may then turn your attention to learning the arm stroke.

The Arm Strokes: The arms should be practised with the face under water, moving the legs only sufficiently to prevent their sinking too low, and to give you the correct position in the water. The arms should be bent at the elbows after they are brought out of the water. The reach should be straight out from the shoulders, placing the hands as far forward as possible before entering the water; by so doing you will conserve your energy. Hold the hands like a scoop; they should be about six inches below the surface before taking the sweep. While doing this the elbows must be perfectly stiff, sweeping the arms with considerable force under the surface as far back as the thighs, the body being propelled forward by the power of this sweep. Swing the arms from the shoulders and just lift them enough to clear the water. Relax the arms at all times excepting when they take the sweep through the water.

Some swimmers draw the arms under the stomach, others use the arms entirely straight, a few place the arms in close to the head and extend to full length under water. As in the

SWIMMING SCIENTIFICALLY TAUGHT

leg stroke, if the pupil tries the different meth-.
ods he will find which one is easiest for him.
Having mastered the arms, combine with the
legs before attempting to breathe, as this in
itself is quite difficult.

Breathing: The breathing must be done entirely through the mouth. On the crawl the

(41) THE CRAWL STROKE—WHEN TO BREATHE

head and not the body must be turned, and just
sufficiently to allow the mouth to come above
the water as the left arm passes the head; a deep
breath can then be taken. When the left arm
comes forward, turn the face under water and
exhale; repeat on every stroke.

Do not raise your head when breathing or
hold your breath for a consecutive number of

strokes. Constant practise will loosen the muscles of the neck, when you will find it much easier. In the trudgen-crawl there is a greater roll to the body, and you breathe when rolling toward the right side, as in Fig. 41.

Having learned the arm and leg movements with the breathing, it is now essential that the position of the body be correct (see Fig. 37). Do not make the mistake of burying your head too deep, or the legs, either; hollow the back so as to present a slight slant to the water. If the legs and back come too high, raise the head a trifle.

THE RACING BACK STROKE

This is a speed stroke and bears a strong resemblance to the crawl. The leg-kick is practically a crawl thrash done on the back, the arms being worked alternately from away behind the head. In fact, the swimmer should reach as far back as possible with each arm out of the water, turning his body slightly to the right for right-arm reach and to the left for left-arm reach, as in the illustration (Figs. 42 and 43). It is a good plan to work on a six-beat thrash, that is, three leg-kicks with each

[103]

arm movement. At the end of each right-arm-pull under water, when the palm of the hand gets to the side of the thigh, exhale and inhale.

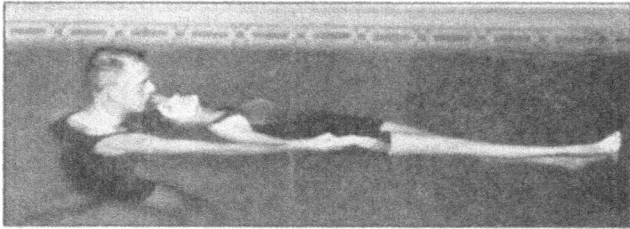

(42) POSITION FOR RACING BACK STROKE

(43) THE RACING BACK STROKE

I have found this racing back stroke and crawl leg practise no strain on the breathing—like lying face down doing the crawl. Very fast time can be made with this stroke for short distances.

[104]

IV

FLOATING, DIVING, AND TRICK SWIMMING

IV

FLOATING, DIVING, AND TRICK SWIMMING

TREADING WATER

TREADING water is a very useful and necessary adjunct to swimming, especially when one falls overboard or goes to the rescue of a drowning person, or when one has to remove one's clothes in the water. In the game of water polo, also, this method of swimming is practised a great deal.

To tread water is like running up-stairs rapidly; the legs have to be brought up and down all the time; the hands should be kept on the surface of the water, the palms continually pressing against the water, and thereby helping the legs to hold the body up.

It is also possible to stand still in deep water, it being merely a question of balance. Stand perfectly still, with the arms in line with the

(44) TREADING WATER

shoulders and the head kept well back in the water. The head will sink below the surface once or twice until the proper balance is reached. When this is attained try breathing through the mouth. The expert can stand still for an indefinite period.

FLOATING

Floating on the surface of the water is enjoyed immensely by all good swimmers. This feat may seem quite simple, but it is not very easily accomplished. There are many persons who are fairly good swimmers, and yet who are unable to float properly. The best of swimmers have often attained this feat only after long and persistent practise. It is possible to learn to float without being able to swim, but in that case only by persons not subject to the least nervousness. As a means of securing rest during exercises in the water, floating gives an ideal position. Without the ability to float one lacks the absolute self-confidence in the water so necessary in order to perform numerous aquatic feats.

[109]

SWIMMING SCIENTIFICALLY TAUGHT

As a rule, women learn to float more quickly than men, because their bones are lighter. Oftentimes women are able to float the first time they enter the water. Strange as it may seem, while this accomplishment is a very dif-

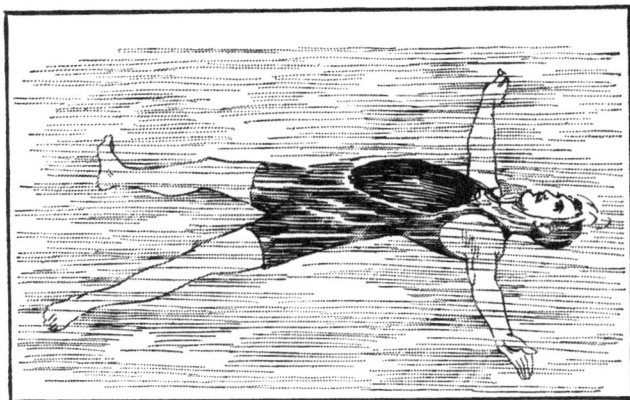

(45) FLOATING POSITION

ficult matter for some men to master, with women it is almost natural. Nothing is more enjoyable to a good swimmer than floating. Especially is this true while bathing at the seashore, when the sea is often rough and the breakers high.

The position for floating is practically the

same as the position for swimming on the back, the only difference being that in floating the body lies perfectly motionless, while in swimming on the back the limbs are constantly in motion. There is no position more comfortable to a swimmer than floating; it is the posi-

(46) INCORRECT FLOATING POSITION

tion of rest, and no bed is so soft as the ocean. To be able to lie perfectly at ease with only the toes peeping above the water is one of many pretty accomplishments in swimming. Yet it requires considerable practise to become perfect in the art.

After the novice has mastered the back stroke, it is essential that he should learn how

[111]

to float in different positions. Begin then by extending the arms above the head, thumbs locked, and back hollowed; then bend slowly backward until the back of the hands and head rest in the water, when, by giving the feet a slight push forward, the legs will rise slowly to

(47) EASY FLOATING POSITION

the surface. Keep the mouth open and breathe deeply, as the more air you have in the lungs the higher the body will float. The head, being the heaviest part of the body in the water, should therefore be kept well back. Should the legs show a tendency to sink, extend the straight-ened out arms under the surface in line with the body above the head; this will counterbal-ance the legs.

[112]

FLOATING, DIVING, TRICK SWIMMING

Another method is to draw the heels up close to the body, spreading the knees wide apart so that the heels will touch each other. Should the body roll from side to side, spread the arms until the body is steadied; sometimes a slight stroke from the side which is rolling is sufficient to maintain the balance. ʻStout persons are

(48) DOUBLE FLOATING

more buoyant than slim ones. Floating in fresh water is more difficult than in salt water. Few male swimmers can float in fresh water at all.

For those who experience this difficulty, I advise double floating with the aid of a friend. Then each supports the other's feet, the first things that sink.

Double Floating: This can be done by two

swimmers, as in the illustration, each with his left hand holding up the other's left ankle. For those who have difficulty in floating, this method is an easy solution of the difficulty. (Fig. 48.)

Triple Floating: The same as double floating, only the swimmer who holds up the feet

(49) TRIPLE FLOATING

of the other two should be a good, buoyant floater. A lady generally fills the bill. (Fig. 49.)

FLOATING, DIVING, TRICK SWIMMING

DIVING

After a person has mastered the first rudiments of swimming, such as the back, breast, side, and crawl strokes, he is naturally anxious to learn to dive. There is nothing more fascinating to a swimmer than a sharp, clean plunge into cool water.

The whole secret of *diving* is the possession of plenty of pluck and self-confidence. One need not be an expert swimmer to be a good diver. In fact, some persons can dive very well and at the same time are mediocre swimmers. As in other branches, practise makes perfect.

While in ordinary swimming diving is indulged in merely for the pleasure derived therefrom, in racing diving is a very important factor. Frequently races are won mainly from the ability of the contender to dive properly; in other words, to get away with a skimming plunge, thus securing a good start and getting into a stride that carries him to victory.

This form of swimming is also of the utmost

(50) TEACHING THE FRONT DIVE

(51) TEACHING THE BACK DIVE

importance in the matter of life-saving. As a luxury in sea-water bathing nothing equals a plunge from a good height.

I advise beginners to practise from a float or springboard, the latter being preferable, as the spring naturally throws the legs up into the air, thereby preventing the diver from landing flat on his stomach, as beginners usually do. The essential points to be considered in diving are to keep the head well tucked in between the extended arms, the thumbs locked, the arms forming an arch above the head. In standing, preparatory to the dive, the knees should be slightly bent, so that the spring comes from the bended knees and toes. Try to stand on the ball of the foot.

In teaching diving to a nervous pupil, at first I generally hold up the left leg as the pupil is bending over to dive (Fig. 50). The farther over he bends, the higher I raise the leg, as shown in the illustration. Then it is impossible for the swimmer to fall flat on the water: the upraised leg prevents that. This is the way that I advise all would-be divers to make their first attempt. After a while the diver will throw up both legs in the air behind him. To

[117]

(52) CORRECT POSITION IN MIDAIR

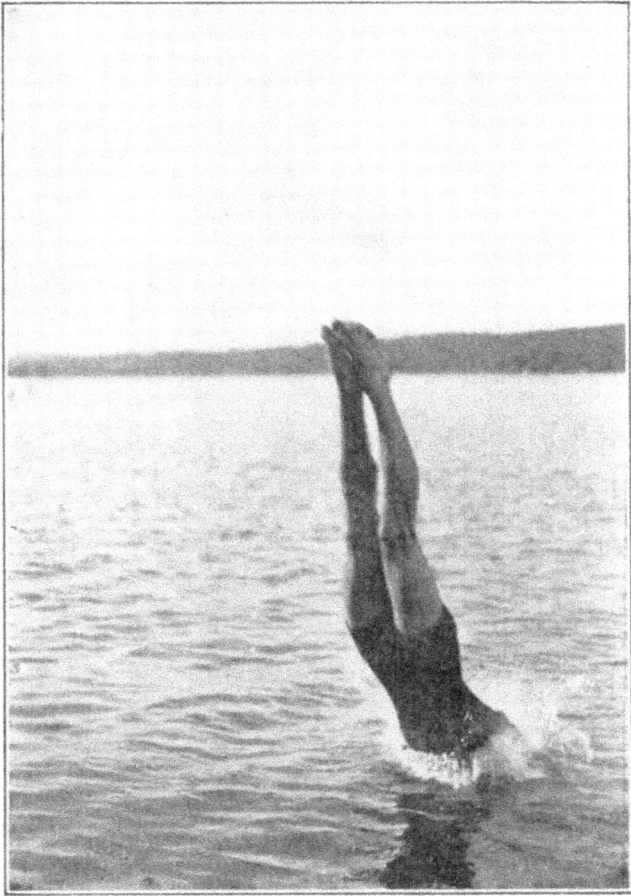

(53) CORRECT POSITION ON ENTERING THE WATER

(54) A BAD DIVE

obviate entering the water with the knees doubled up, as so many do (see Fig. 54), the toes must be pointed straight up, back arched. Pointing the toes tends to straighten the legs out. Another method I use is to hold a long stick across the water, about four feet away and three feet above the diving-board. This makes the diver spring well out and throw his legs up behind him. It is well for the diver always to keep his thumbs interlocked. Otherwise, if he should be diving in a shallow place, the hands would spread and the head would strike bottom; locking the thumbs prevents this.

A *deep dive* should be made from the edge of the pool or from the diving-board, bending the knees slightly, keeping the head tucked in well between the extended arms, thumbs locked, springing up and entering the water as close to the take-off as possible. On a *shallow dive,* shoot out as far as possible, keeping the head well down; directly hands and head are under water, turn hands up and hollow the back. After practise, hands are out of the water again before toes are under water.

After deep and shallow dives have been mas-

(55) MRS. FRANK EUGEN DALTON IN POSITION FOR A DIVE

tered, the pupil can take up fancy diving. It is best to work up from the simple to the intricate dives. Let us start on the side dive.

The *side dive* is made by standing sideways on the diving-board, the forward foot turned so that the toes grip the edge of the board. When springing out, the back should be well hollowed and the face turned up, the head well tucked in between the arms.

The *back dive* requires a depth of at least six feet. The toes should be well up to the edge of the pool and the back well hollowed. This is the main essential; one also must point the toes out well, and not try to spring. Keeping the feet well down hollows the back and prevents over-balancing in the air.

The *front somersault dive* is another interesting one. It is done by taking two steps, jumping to the end of the board, and springing well up in the air. Double body at waist in midair, keeping the head well tucked down, and work your body around so that you land feet first when entering the water (Fig. 57).

The *back somersault* is executed by springing back and doubling body at waist, with head forward. Work the body around in the

(56) THE BACK DIVE

[124]

air, keeping hands and arms well in to the body. Turn enough so that you land in the water feet first, with hands at sides (Fig. 58).

The *jack-knife dive* is spectacular but not at all difficult. It is done by taking two steps and a jump at the end of the board and doubling your body in midair at the height of the spring. In doing this, try to touch your shins with your fingers, and your legs will automatically come up. The only thing you must watch out for in the front jack-knife is to spring high enough so that you will have plenty of time in midair to execute this dive (Fig. 59).

The *back jack-knife* is not so easy to learn. However, it is simple enough to execute once you grasp the principle. In this dive you should stand with your heels on the edge of the board. Hold your hands out in front of you and arch your back. Then throw your arms up, swing them back, and spring. The arm swing will pull the body away from the spring-board, and your spring backward will throw your legs up, so that you enter the water in a straightened position. Your fingers must touch the shins in the air, and then the back-jack will be easily accomplished (Fig. 60).

(57) RUNNING FRONT SOMERSAULT

(58) BACK SOMERSAULT

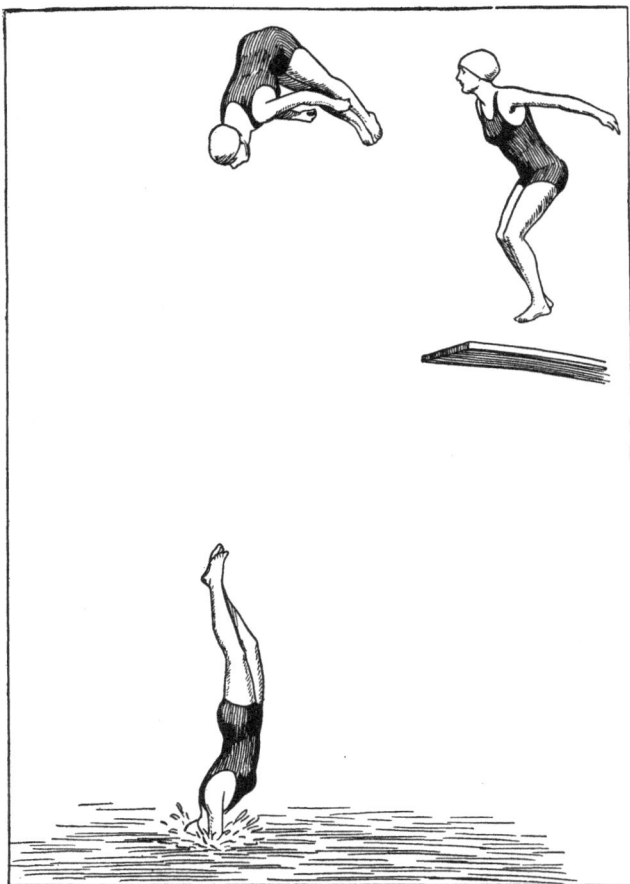

(59) RUNNING FRONT JACK-KNIFE DIVE

(60) BACK JACK-KNIFE DIVE

(61) SWAN DIVE

[130]

(62) THE STANDING-SITTING DIVE

(63) THE NECK DIVE

(64) TWIST OR CORKSCREW DIVE

(65) HAND-STAND DIVE

(66) THE FLYING DUTCHMAN

SWIMMING SCIENTIFICALLY TAUGHT

The *swan dive* is exceedingly graceful and is not nearly as difficult to accomplish as it looks to the spectator. Stand in regular straight-away diving position. Spring forward strongly with toes pointed. Then throw your arms back, bend back, arch your body and just before contact with the water bring your arms forward and tuck your head into regular diving position (Fig. 61).

The next dive is the *standing-sitting dive*. Poise on tiptoe on the edge of the board. Sit down hard. By bending knees the impact will throw legs up if you hold your head down. The legs should be spread apart to clear the board at each side and brought together in the air, so that you strike the water in the regular diving position with hands extended. A lot of people in learning this dive would like to put a nice, big, soft cushion on the end of the board, but, honestly, you do not land on the board, when you sit, half as hard as the noise of the impact leads spectators to believe.

In the *standing-sitting-standing dive* from a standing position the diver assumes a sitting position as in a *sitting dive,* drawing the knees under to regain the feet again and pushing off for the dive. To add to the brilliancy of this dive, when regaining your footing on the board after sitting, turn a forward somersault instead of diving in head first (Fig. 62).

The *neck dive* must be done from a spring-board well above the water. Grip the front of the board with the hands, with the head well over the edge, throwing the legs in the air, turning the body over, and back somersaulting into the water, feet first (Fig. 63).

The *twist* or *corkscrew dive* is done by springing straight out and giving your body a short twist to the right. The *half twist* makes the body enter the water in the position of the back dive. The *full twist* makes you enter the water in the position of the front dive (Fig. 64).

The next to learn is the *head-stand dive*. Put your hands and head on the edge of the board, throw one leg up and try to balance on your head, then overbalance, keeping back well hollowed, at the same time pushing with your hands on the edge of the board so that you will enter the water feet first.

The *hand-stand dive* is similar, only it takes more strength to support the body on the arms. The difference is that in this dive you must

[137]

actually stand balanced on your head before hollowing your back, overbalancing, pushing away from the board, and entering the water hands first (Fig. 65).

The Flying Dutchman: This difficult dive should be learned in easy stages. First practise springing well up from the board, hands above head, using the two steps and jump to end of board to get a good take-off. The next stage is to spring well up and force the feet up in front of you, toes pointed. The final stage consists of springing well up in the air, forcing the feet up in front of you, throwing the arms well back and down, hollowing the back, the same as in the back dive, and going into the water hands first. Don't spring too far out, or control will be lost. Be deliberate. Just make three movements—the up-spring, the raising of the feet in front, and the back dive (Fig. 66).

When a swimmer has improved and added speed to his racing stroke, he should practise shallow racing dives and the trick of *turning sharply* in a tank. This is very important, as many a race has been lost through the inability of the racer to turn sharply when reaching the end of a tank. To practise this, swim slowly to the end of the tank; gage your strokes so that the right hand grasps the bar which is usually placed around the tank a little above the water. Throw the left arm over the right arm against the marble side of the bath under water; at the same time double the body up, switch around, gathering yourself well together, and shoot forward with the arms extended. Ten to twenty feet can be covered on a good push-off. The method usually followed by swimmers in America is to double up and turn to the left when they are within a foot of the end of the bath without touching with the hands, but pushing off with the feet. In races in England this turn is not allowed, as the racer must touch the end of the bath with his hands.

A *racing dive* is a very shallow dive. The quicker the swimmer gets to the surface the less time he wastes in getting into his stroke. Both are very important and should be well practised. When training in a tank, the racer should never go the full distance, but reserve his speed for the day of the race. In a tank it is a good plan to count the number of strokes required to do the length, so that you know just when the end of the bath is reached without turning the head. A straight course is always advisable. This can be kept by swimming parallel with the side of the bath. It is good practise to get a friend to time your lengths, and get used to diving at the word "go." The best position for a racing dive is with the hands in front of the body, the knees bent, and the mouth open, so that you get all the air possible before striking the water. Always spring out as far as you can. Never mind if it is a flat dive. This is much better than a deep, clean dive, and less time is lost.

The dives I have mentioned are the basis for all other fancy dives, such as the one-and-a-half somersault, the front and back half-twist jack, the full twist, the double somersault, the seal, the back-sitting, the turtle, and so forth. In teaching, as we do, dozens of people every day, we have found one point which is good advice for every one. If you are trying to make a dive and you land badly, go right back and do it over again. In other words, don't stop diving with a poor dive, or you may find that you are just a little bit afraid to try it over again the next time you practise.

FLOATING, DIVING, TRICK SWIMMING

SWIMMING LIKE A DOG

Children generally manage to swim like a dog in their initial attempts. This is a very

(67) SWIMMING LIKE A DOG

easy and simple method of propulsion, mainly for the reason that the arms and legs are never lifted above water.

Legs are kicked out straight to the rear, sole of each foot striking the water squarely and alternately, instead of working together.

SWIMMING SCIENTIFICALLY TAUGHT

Hands are placed in front of the body, with palms down, and are successively brought down under the body and up again.

PLUNGING

To become a good plunger the swimmer, first of all, has to have good lungs. He must be able to hold his breath for at least one minute under water. Ability to float face down, as in the dead man's float, is also essential. Many would-be plungers find that their feet sink after having gone about a dozen yards, the reason being lack of practise in floating.

When practising for plunging the take-off should be about three feet above the water. The thumbs should be locked, the knees slightly bent, and the edge of the pool-wall gript well with the toes. Empty the lungs by exhaling, then fill again with a long, deep breath, and at the last inhalation spring forward, with all the force possible, taking care not to go deep in the water; about two feet down is sufficient. Keep the head well down and the toes pointing up. The back should be arched and the legs bent up from the knees; this will counteract the tendency of the legs to sink. Unless one makes a straight dive by pushing off equally strong with both legs, the body will go sideways to the

(68) CORRECT POSITION FOR LONG PLUNGE

side of the pool. Floating on the back or chest is mainly a question of balance, and comes only after considerable practise.

The time limit allowed in a plunge is 60 seconds without raising the face out of the water. The record is over 81 feet, 5 inches, and was made in England by H. W. Allason.

SCULLING -

This is one of the simplest methods of swimming on the back, the forearms and hands alone being in motion during the performance. The swimmer turns on the back with the legs straight out and together, or crossed, the arms being flexible and near the body. The hands, with palms downward, must be in line with the thighs, with the fingers slightly raised. The hands are worked from the wrists, from right to left, in addition to a slight movement (right to left) of the forearm. This forces the body, head first, very gracefully through the water.

SWIMMING BACKWARD ON THE CHEST

In this trick of swimming backward on the chest, the body is placed in position as in the breast stroke, the legs and arms together, outstretched in line with the body. The feet must be moved slowly from the knees, each leg separately. The feet are alternately pushed backward and the toes extended to the rear. The feet must not come above the water. The action of the hands is performed with the palms facing outward, each hand being pushed alternately forward.

Another method of using the hands is the

(69) SWIMMING BACKWARD ON CHEST

reverse of the breast-stroke movement; in other words, the breast-stroke movement is done backward.

Begin with the arms out straight in front, the palms together, and then draw the arms backward until the wrists touch the chest. Next throw out the arms horizontally in line with the shoulders, the palms turned out, thus send-

[145]

ing the body backward by bringing the outstretched arms straight together until the palms
touch. If the performer be an expert swimmer
he can, by using this arm movement, dispense
with the leg movements. This is a "stunt" well
worth practising, as it looks very effective in
the water.

THE WASHING TUB

This is a very simple performance and
requires little practise. The swimmer turns on

(70) THE WASHING TUB

his back, doubles the body by bringing the knees up to the chin, with the legs crossed. The body is kept in position by working the hands the same as in sculling. As soon as the swimmer has obtained his balance, he pushes the water away from his body with the right hand and uses the left hand in the opposite manner, or, as it were, pulls the water toward the body with the left hand (Fig. 70).

THE PROPELLER

This is a very graceful movement and never fails to excite admiration in onlookers. To do it properly requires considerable practise. One must be able to float well. There is always a tendency to raise the head above the proper level, which in turn causes the feet to sink.

To begin, the swimmer should turn on the back, placing the hands at the side of the body, keeping the head back and the feet together. Slight movements of the hands from the wrists will keep the body floating. Then make a long sweep of the arms from the body, under the surface of the water, until they are at full

SWIMMING SCIENTIFICALLY TAUGHT

length beyond the head. Thus the body will be propelled with the feet foremost. As soon as the body is in motion, the hands should be moved by the wrists and forearms only, in a scoop-like manner, with the palms turned outward. The body may be turned round by les-

(71) THE PROPELLER

sening the movement of one hand and increasing that of the other, the body turning to the side on which the lesser movement is taking place. Bringing the arms to the side again as in the original position will bring the body to a standstill. This trick, seemingly very simple, is somewhat difficult of accomplishment, and requires considerable practise (Fig. 71).

[148]

THE TORPEDO

This is a rather difficult performance. It requires a great deal of practise (Fig. 72). The movements are almost identical with those

(72) THE TORPEDO

in the "propeller," the main difference being that in this trick the head is kept under water.

To begin, the performer should lie flat in the water on his back, with his arms stretched out beyond his head. The palms should be turned upward. Then the legs should be

[149]

raised from the hips, and kept rigid. This will cause the body to become submerged, all but the ankles and feet. One then must work the hands the same as in "propeller," but at the end of each stroke make a slight upward pressure with the palms, so that the body may retain its position below the water.

The movement of the hands will cause the body to move forward, feet first. The swimmer should at all times keep his eyes open in order to guide himself in a straight line.

THE CATHERINE WHEEL

This is a very effective "stunt." After assuming the floating position, turn on the right side, with the arms at full length, the hands close to the body, and the knees drawn up. Begin by moving the legs sideways; that is, bring each knee up alternately, straightening out the legs and making a wide sweep with each leg before bringing it up again. The legs are used the same as paddles on a side-wheeler (Fig. 73). This should be practised on both sides. One hand is made to scoop the

FLOATING, DIVING, TRICK SWIMMING

water toward the body in front, while the other
is manipulated the same way at the back. With

(73) THE CATHERINE WHEEL

a little practise one thus may simulate a Catherine wheel—at least when the act is done rapidly
and efficiently.

ROLLING

To roll in the water one has to be able to
float well; to roll easily the body must float as

high in the water as possible. No movements of arms or legs are required at all, the balancing being done with the head.

First get into a floating position, the arms extended beyond the head, the ankles crossed as in Fig. 74. Then fill the lungs well with air,

(74) ROLLING

and gently rock the body from side to side, increasing the motion until the body rolls nearly over on its side. Having reached this position, turn the face well over on the right side, and the body will roll over and turn up again on the other side. After the first complete roll, once momentum is started, the second becomes easier. Several rolls can be made before stopping, provided the breath holds out. Always finish in the floating position. When one has learned how to roll over on the right side, rolling on the left side should be practised, until that movement becomes as easy as the other one. After practise the rolls can be made very easily and gracefully, without splashing. The legs must always be kept crossed and together, never letting the hands come out of the water.

SWIMMING LIKE A PORPOISE

This trick, very interesting and pretty, is quite mirth-provoking to the onlooker, especially if indulged in by a number of swimmers. Unlike the vast majority of tricks performed in the water, it does not call for ability to float well, the only qualification being that one must be a fairly good swimmer (Fig. 75).

Begin by lying flat on the water with the face downward. Then, with the head out of the water, take a deep inspiration after having cleared the lungs. As the chest begins to inflate, the body must be allowed to sink under water. At the end of the inspiration the head

(75) SWIMMING LIKE A PORPOISE

should go below the surface. After a couple
of breast strokes under water, turn the head
upward. By executing a strong kick with the
legs, the head will rise out of the water. As
the body rises, make one stroke with the arms,
and, as soon as the head comes up, the arms
should be recovered to the first position of the
breast stroke and pushed together downward
through the water from its level to the side of
the body. Simultaneously, as the hands are
moving toward the body, the legs should be
straightened with a sharp kick. This will force
the head and shoulders out of the water.

A sudden inclination of the head toward
the chest will assist the body in rolling over,
when the back and legs will become visible
after the head is again under water, the legs
being the last to sink. By carefully regulating
the breathing, this momentum can be effected
a number of times.

THE PENDULUM

This is another very clever trick, requiring
considerable practise; the main essential is abil-

ity to float. The "pendulum" is primarily a balancing feat, a well-inflated chest being the chief requisite.

The body should first be allowed to float on the water, with the arms stretched out beyond the head and in line with the body. The head must be thrown well back while the body is kept perfectly still. Then take a deep inhalation, bringing the head well forward, as if to look at the feet. Simultaneously with this movement draw hands toward the head. These combined movements will cause the body to sink, and thus assume a perpendicular position in the water (Fig. 76).

When the body has assumed a perpendicular position, the arms must be brought to the front of the body, stretched well out, and at the same time the head must be sunk between the arms until the face and arms lie on the surface of the water. When the arms and head are down, the feet will rise and the body float on the surface with the face down.

To come back to the first position, the head must be tilted backward and the hands drawn to the back of the head. Again the feet will sink and the body be swung back to a perpen-

(76) THE PENDULUM

dicular position with the face above water. One must then stretch the arms at full length behind the head, with the palms upward, gradually inclining the head backward until the legs once more rise to the surface, and the body floats face upward.

Repetition of these movements produces a swinging similar to that of a pendulum. The movements must be accomplished with regularity, at all times keeping the legs straight and together.

THE SOMERSAULT

This is one of the easiest and simplest of tricks. With very little practise it can be mastered by most ordinary swimmers. Of course, this statement refers to the ordinary somersault, either backward or forward, which is nothing more than a turning over of the body while in the water.

In the back somersault the head is tilted back as far as possible, the legs well drawn up, and the arms thrown out horizontally from the shoulders. Then the body is turned on the back and a stroke taken with the arms and hands. As the body is doubled up, this action causes it to turn completely over, the head going under first.

In the forward somersault, the head is pressed down upon the chest, the legs doubled

(77) FORWARD SOMERSAULT

up, the same as in the back somersault, the arms at right angles with the body, and the palms downward. The stroke is made similar to that in the back somersault, but the movement is started in front (Fig. 77).

If there are a number of these motions to be made, the lungs should be well filled before beginning, as there is no time for proper breathing.

DOUBLE SOMERSAULTS

As this trick requires two swimmers, it makes necessary a great deal more practise. To begin, the swimmers stand on the bottom of the pool, one in front of the other. The forward swimmer throws out his arms at right angles with the body, even with the shoulders, and spreads his legs until his feet are about twelve inches apart. Then the second swimmer, after taking a deep breath, dives under water and places his head between the legs of the other, bending his legs backward until they come close to the head of the forward swimmer, who in turn tilts his head backward so that it may be grasped by the legs of the other (Fig. 78).

When in this position, the swimmers begin to turn backward, using the arms the same as in the backward (single) somersault. The head of each swimmer should be tilted well backward. As the head of the forward swimmer disappears below the surface, the head of the other should appear. After several turns the grip of the legs may be released and the swimmers rise to the surface in their original positions.

(78) DOUBLE SOMERSAULT

WITH ONE LEG OUT OF WATER

In this act the swimmer should lie on his
back, the same as in sculling, and raise one
leg until it is at right angles with the body,

(79) ONE LEG OUT OF WATER

keeping the other leg straight and rigid.   The
action of the hands will propel the body forward (Fig. 79).

When becoming proficient in this movement, the swimmer can practise raising the
other leg.   This requires considerably more
force in the working of the hands, so that both

legs may be kept in position. By performing the motion of the hands directly under the legs, less difficulty will be experienced.

SWIMMING WITH CLOTHES ON

This is an accomplishment that should be learned by all swimmers. In addition to the sense of security given in time of accident, it is productive of great amusement at race meets and exhibitions, and never fails to excite admiration and wonder in the onlooker. Of course, this can be practised with an old or cast-off suit.

Practise first with a coat, then with a coat and vest; next add the trousers, and last the shoes and socks. This will gradually accustom the beginner to the extra weight of the clothes.

In case of an immersion in clothes, with no help in sight, the sooner the swimmer removes his clothes the longer he can support himself. The easiest way is to float on the back and remove the coat, taking out one arm at a time, using the legs as in the Dalton stroke; next remove the vest, still lying on the back; then unbutton the trousers and pull the right leg down with the left hand. To remove the left leg, use the left hand and kick out with the right leg. To remove the shoes, lie on the back and draw up one leg at a time, crossed over the other leg, and so try and undo the laces. If a knife is handy, cut the laces and kick the shoes off. This is one of the most effective feats practised at exhibitions.

WITH HANDS AND FEET TIED

This trick is most frequently performed with the wrists and ankles tied with a rope. The performer should plunge into the water as for a shallow dive and rise to the surface without making a stroke. The legs are then drawn up until the heels are quite close to the back of the thighs, then the legs are kicked out together. The arms are drawn down through the water, in front of the body, and then shot out. Care must be taken that too much force be not employed, or much of the beauty of this movement will be lost.

FLOATING, DIVING, TRICK SWIMMING

Naturally, the pace will be slow, but this does not detract from its neatness, nor lessen the admiration that this trick always calls forth.

This feat is often performed by experts with their arms tied to their sides or behind their backs. When performing in this manner, one must swim on the back, and the legs only can be used for propulsion. In this instance better progress is made, as it is much easier to swim on the back with the hands and feet tied than it is to swim on the breast under the same conditions. The main essential to the performance of this trick is ability to float. Also, these performances are much easier in a tidal river or stream than in still water, as the body is carried forward with the motion of the water, and less exertion is necessary to remain on the surface.

OVER AND UNDER

This is one of the prettiest exhibition tricks that can be accomplished in the water. If performed by a lady and gentleman it never fails to elicit great applause. The swimmers

SWIMMING SCIENTIFICALLY TAUGHT

begin with floating alongside of each other. Then one slowly paddles ahead of the other with his hands until his toes are in line with the shoulders of the other. When in that position, the first grasps the neck of the other with his toes. Then the other slowly brings his or her arms back under water and catches hold of the ankles of the first. After balancing for a moment, the other dips his or her head below the surface, at the same time giving a strong pull at the ankles of the first, which draws the first directly over him. The first one allows his arms to float straight behind him. While the first is slowly sailing over the other submerged, the latter watches the former, and when the neck of the first is in line with the feet of the other, the latter raises his feet and grasps the neck of the former, who allows his body to rise to the surface. The performance is then repeated by the first grasping the ankles of the other, and continuing as before (Fig. 80).

These movements must be done slowly and gracefully, each swimmer allowing the other time to inflate the lungs before the next pull-over is made. After these movements have

[167]

been gone through about a dozen times, and when in position for the final pull, the forward one should loosen the grip on the neck and propel himself ahead to the side of the other swimmer, when both can bend forward in unison, making a very neat and graceful finale.

SWIMMING UNDER WATER

To be able to swim under water is quite an accomplishment and often may be of very valuable service, but as an achievement in competition or for exhibition purposes it is not to be encouraged because of the danger of prolonged immersion, and the fact that many competitors do not know when to stop.

Under-water swimming should be practised by experts only, and care must be taken not to prolong the immersion in order to reach a definite point or to accomplish a certain distance before rising to the surface. It often happens that swimmers, in order to achieve a certain distance, remain under water after *pains in the back of the neck give warning of oncoming unconsciousness,* in which case they may lapse into a state of insensibility, and there is grave danger of drowning.

When these contests take place in baths, it is not a pleasant sight to watch a swimmer struggling on, against odds, in the hope of beating a rival for the coveted prize. The action of the arms and legs becomes slower and slower, until at last, from sheer exhaustion, the body rises toward the surface for a short distance and then sinks to the bottom motionless.

One of the advantages of being able to swim under water is the ability it imparts to the swimmer to reach the body of a drowning person, or to bring the body of a drowned person to the surface.

In swimming under water, the ordinary breast stroke is the one used. To swim downward, the head is pressed down toward the breast, and when wishing to rise the head is deflected backward.

If swimming under water for a long distance, the body should be kept near the surface, for the reason that the pressure is greater in the corresponding depth. Care should be taken to fill the lungs before starting, and as soon as the first symptoms of asphyxiation are noticeable, the swimmer should rise to the surface.

Among the notable feats accomplished under water may be mentioned that of James Finney, in England, in 1882, who accomplished a distance of 340 feet. William Reilly, of Salford, an amateur, swam 312 feet under water.

The time limit for under-water swimming is about a minute and a half. At the Crystal Palace, London, England, in 1892, in a diver's tank fifteen feet deep, I succeeded in picking up seventy-four plates in a single immersion.

MONTE CRISTO SACK TRICK

This is one of the most sensational performances of the professional swimmer. From a spectacular point of view it is very effective. To do this trick one must be an adept at under-water swimming; an assistant is necessary in order to tie the knots properly.

The sack to be used must be large enough to allow plenty of room for the swimmer to move about in it. At the bottom of the sack a number of heavy weights are placed. At the top, where it is to be tied, a concealed hole must be cut, through which a rope can be passed. (See

(81) MONTE CRISTO SACK TRICK

Fig. 81.) The trick lies in the fact that what looks like one piece of rope, used to tie the top of the sack securely, is really two separate and parallel pieces, with two ends inside the sack and the other two ends outside

[171]

SWIMMING SCIENTIFICALLY TAUGHT

The swimmer gets into the sack, taking firm
hold of the loose ends of rope that are inside, at
the same time grasping the top of the sack
above his head near where it is to be tied. The
assistant then takes hold of the two outside
rope-ends and ties them tightly together—on
the side opposite to that on which the swimmer
is grasping them inside. To the spectator it
now looks as if the sack were tightly tied,
whereas the assistant has only tied two loose
pieces of rope together. The moment the swimmer releases them inside, he can pull both pieces,
knot and all, through the hole, thus leaving the
sack wide open. The same results can be obtained with a single piece of rope, doubled in the
middle. The doubled part is passed through
the single hole and grasped by the swimmer,
while the ends, outside, are tied together by the
assistant. When the swimmer releases the
loop inside, it is drawn through the hole as he
forces the sack open.

After warning the swimmer, so that he may
inflate his lungs, the assistant throws him, sack
and all, into the deep water. The weights cause
him to sink feet first. In a few seconds he
releases the rope and pushes the sack open with

FLOATING, DIVING, TRICK SWIMMING

his hands, thus becoming free to rise to the surface.

This appears to be a dangerous feat, but if carefully managed it is in reality a very simple one for a good swimmer.

V

ACQUIRING SPEED AND ENDURANCE

V

ACQUIRING SPEED AND ENDURANCE

LONG DISTANCE SWIMMING

ANYONE who knows how to swim can become a long distance swimmer. It is mainly a matter of practise, and of understanding what strokes to employ and how to use them. In the case of people in middle life, I always advise preliminary practise for long distance swimming. They haven't the vigor to go tearing out on the crawl strokes the way the youngsters do; it's like a strenuous match of tennis in that it's too exhausting.

I do not want these older people, however, to get the impression that long distance swimming is too much for them, for it is not. People who can go out and play thirty-six holes of golf a day, as the golf fans do, can also take up long distance swimming without discomfort. With a little practise you can swim for an hour or two with no dangerous amount of exertion. Young people likewise can take up distance swimming with unfailing profit and enjoyment.

It's all very well to be able to speed up, but the tendency to-day seems to be too much for speed. Among the younger element, a lot of the crawl stroke advocates are exhausted after covering a distance of a hundred yards. After all, speed is only a small part of the fun you can get out of the water.

The secret of long distance swimming is to conserve the strength and energy, thus obtaining every inch of distance from every ounce of energy expended. To swim far, four different strokes should be developed. The right and left side stroke, the overarm, the breast, and the back strokes are those best adapted for the purpose. I say four strokes advisedly, because they enable one to shift around, and not become tired too quickly through the monotony of going through the same motion over and over again.

Long distance swimming is a matter of constant practise. As in walking or any other form of exercise, when you start in you can't go very far before you become tired. But if you determine, each time you go out, to swim a little farther and a little longer than the time before, you will be surprized at the distance you are able to cover.

In practising for this kind of work it is not at all necessary to swim straight away from the shore for miles. You can practise long distance swimming in a pool. Simply turn at each end and keep on swimming. Of course, it is better to work in a more lengthy space if such is available, but don't overexert yourself by swimming out a great distance only to become too exhausted to swim back. It is always safer to have somebody accompany you in a boat, with a rope ladder hooked to the stern or side to enable you to get out of the water, instead of having to raise your body over the side of the boat when tired or suffering from cramps.

There are both enjoyment and good exercise in being able to swim a few miles when one feels like it. This kind of swimming is probably the finest form of drill that one can give the human body. Every muscle is brought into play. You are not overexerting or overstraining at any time, and in many ways it is far easier than walking steadily for the same period. Of

[179]

course, this applies only to those who have practised and become physically fit. A good point to remember is not to eat too much before you start.

When my father swam the English Channel he always rested by spread-eagling and floating, also eating and drinking in that position, from a bottle and tube. While training for that Channel swim in 1890, his daily practise stunt was a swim of four to seven miles, with a brisk rub-down with oil before and after. Also he used a woollen swimming suit and cap made especially to protect his head and ears from the cold Channel water. The average long distance swimmer must be well covered with flesh to stand the temperature; a slim person feels the cold too much, and the body once chilled is hard to keep going. Long daily walks, with deep breathing, are a great help to long distance swimming; the deeper the lung capacity the better the body floats and the higher one swims, with resultant easier propulsion through the water.

Just go into the water and take it easy, resting as long as possible after each stroke. Develop your leg kick and your arm motion sep-

ACQUIRING SPEED AND ENDURANCE

arately, so that you can rest your legs and swim only with your arms, or vice versa. After a reasonable amount of training you will find yourself a master of the finest health-giving sport ever invented, to say nothing of having acquired a valuable kind of life insurance in cases of emergency.

SUCCESSFUL CHANNEL SWIMS

Considerable interest was aroused in the early part of August, 1875, when the statement was made that Captain Matthew Webb, an Englishman who had served as second mate on several ships in the Indian and North Atlantic trade, intended to attempt the remarkable feat of swimming across the English Channel. His first attempt resulted in failure. This took place on August 12, 1875. After swimming for 6 hours 48 minutes and 30 seconds, during which period he covered 13½ miles, Webb was compelled to leave the water, as he had drifted 9¾ miles to the eastward of his course, owing to a northeast stream and stress of weather. Webb started from Dover

2 hours 25 minutes before high water on a tide rising 13 feet 7 inches at that port. When he gave up no estimate could be formed as to the probable distance he would have gone west on the tide.

In his second and successful attempt, on August 24 of the same year, Webb started from Dover 3¼ hours before high water on a 15-foot 10-inch tide, which gave him one hour and three-quarters of the southwest stream. His point of landing was 21½ miles from Dover, as the crow flies, but the actual length of the swim was 39½ miles. Very little rest was taken by Webb on the way. When he did stop it was to take refreshment, and then he was treading water. During the whole time he had no recourse to artificial aids. The temperature of the water was about 65 degrees. Webb never complained of cold.

For the first 15 hours the weather was fine. The sea was as smooth as glass, the sun obscured during the day by a haze, so that the heat did not affect Webb's head, and in the night a three-quartered moon lighted him on his way. The worst time began at 3 A. M. on August 25th, as drowsiness had to be overcome and rough water was entered. At this hour he was only some 4½ miles off Cape Gris Nez, France, and altho he was not then strong enough to strike out a direct course athwart the new northeast stream for land, he was fetching well in for Sangatte, where he would undoubtedly have landed between 7 and 8 A. M. had adverse weather not set in. He finally landed on the Calais Sands after having been in the water 21 hours 45 minutes. After performing this feat, Webb for some years gave exhibitions of diving and swimming at an aquarium in London and elsewhere. In July, 1883, he came to America for the purpose of swimming the rapids and whirlpool at Niagara, and in this attempt lost his life.

On August 17-18, 1890, Captain Dalton left Sandgate for Boulogne with the intention of swimming back across the Channel to Folkestone, a distance of 27 miles. Dalton expressed his conviction that he could perform the journey in 20 hours, and if successful would beat the time of Captain Webb. He entered the water at 6 P. M. on Sunday and accomplished the journey, without any remarkable incident, at 5.45 P. M. the following day.

SWIMMING SCIENTIFICALLY TAUGHT

William T. Burgess, of Yorkshire, England, crossed the English Channel in 1911 from South Foreland, Dover, England, to La Chatelet, two miles east of Cape Gris Nez, France. Burgess started at 11.15 A. M., September 5, 1911, and finished at 9.50 A. M., September 6. Time, 22 hours 35 minutes. The distance is 40 miles. Burgess is said to have covered nearly 60 miles, owing to changes in the tide and currents.

After 1911 no swimmers conquered the English Channel until 1923, which was a banner year. Three then accomplished the feat. Henry Sullivan, of Lowell, Mass., swam from Dover to Cape Gris Nez in 27 hours, 23 minutes. Enrico Tirabocchi, an Italo-Argentinean, swam from Cape Gris Nez to Dover Sands in 16 hours, 33 minutes, beating all previous records. Charles Toth, of Boston, swam from Cape Gris Nez to Dover in 16 hours, 54 minutes.

Three more years elapsed before the Channel was again conquered, and this time—in the summer of 1926—two of the supposed weaker sex not only accomplished the seemingly impossible swim, but both beat the record: Mrs

ACQUIRING SPEED AND ENDURANCE

Clemington Corson by 1 hour and 5 minutes, Miss Gertrude Ederle by 2 hours and 2 minutes. The outstanding achievements of 1926 were as follows:

Miss Gertrude Ederle, New York's record-breaker, swam on August 7-8 from Cape Gris Nez to the English shore at Kingsdown, near Dover, in 14 hours and 31 minutes.

Mrs. Clemington Corson, an American, on August 28-29, swam from Cape Gris Nez to the Dover Sands in 15 hours and 28 minutes.

Ernest Vierkoetter, a German, on August 30-31, swam from Cape Gris Nez to the English shore near Dover in 12 hours, 43 minutes, beating all previous records.

Georges Michel, a Frenchman, on Sept. 10-11, swam from Cape Gris Nez to St. Margaret's Bay, near Dover, in 11 hours, 43 minutes, again lowering the Channel record.

Norman Leslie Derham, an Englishman, swam the Channel at the same place on Sept. 16-17, in 13 hours, 57 minutes.

Cape Gris Nez was the favorite starting point for Channel swimmers in 1926, as the currents favored starting from the French side.

I attribute the lowering of the Channel

record to two things: First, getting over on three instead of four tides, and secondly, the using of speedier strokes, such as the double overarm, the trudgen, and the trudgen-crawl. It would be impossible to cover the distance on the straight crawl, as the leg thrash is too tiring for distances of more than a mile, but the trudgen-kick with a combination scissors can be kept up indefinitely. I expect the Channel swim to be lowered to ten hours. It has already come close to this mark. On June 9, 1927, Venceslas Spacek, a newspaper mechanic of Prague, Bohemia, swam from a point on the French Coast between Calais and Cape Gris Nez, to Dover, England, in 10 hours and 45 minutes. The Channel was conquered four times in that year and three times in the next, several of the swimmers being women; but none came anywhere near Spacek's record for speed.

Another record-breaking feat of long-distance swimming was that of George Young, a seventeen-year-old youth of Toronto, Canada, who on January 15-16, 1927, swam across the San Pedro Channel from Catalina Island to the California shore in 15 hours and 44 minutes, thereby winning the $25,000 prize offered by

ACQUIRING SPEED AND ENDURANCE

William Wrigley, Jr. The Channel is twenty-two miles wide, but Young probably covered thirty miles in crossing. Out of 102 men and women who tried for the prize, he was the only one who completed this difficult swim in the chilly Pacific waters. Five times he changed his course to meet the opposition of tidal currents, the worst of which had to be fought when he was within a mile and a quarter of shore. The stroke that carried him to victory was the trudgen-crawl.

VI

KEEPING FIT BY SWIMMING

VI

KEEPING FIT BY SWIMMING

AS A HEALTH EXERCISE

WHEN you swim, practically every muscle in your body is brought into play. The muscles of the abdomen, calf and thighs are developed and strengthened by the leg kick on the back stroke and side strokes. The muscles of the back, chest and arms are brought into play with the arm movement, and for those who want more strenuous exercise I recommend a half-mile to a mile swim every day with the double-overarm, trudgen or crawl stroke.

The double advantage of exercising by swimming is that the weight of the body is supported by the water and taken off the feet. This is a particular advantage to stout people, for there is no other form of exercise which is so thorough, and which yet eliminates the overstrain on the heart caused by supporting their weight.

And what is there to equal the physical exhilaration of swimming? All lassitude disappears as one strikes out, feeling better and stronger with each stroke. There is a sense of pure enjoyment in the contact of crystal clear water—a sense of freedom and power—a deep delight in the sweep of the strokes.

Well may the onlooker envy the swimmer who dives in, swims under water about thirty feet, comes to the surface, and starts right out on the breast stroke with strong arm-sweeps and powerful leg-kicks, driving himself at a good speed to the end of the pool, making a turn, and coming back on the side stroke. On the next length he turns to the trudgen, after which, to give himself a rest, he drops into the back stroke, then finishes up with a couple of fast lengths on the trudgen-crawl. Could anything be more exhilarating or enjoyable, summer or winter?

I know of no better way of getting concentrated exercise, than by swimming four hundred yards three times weekly. It is just the thing for the average business man or woman

KEEPING FIT BY SWIMMING

with limited time for exercise. The deep breathing helps to exercise the abdominal muscles.

A good way of exercising is to swim regularly with a friend. This keeps up the interest in trying to outswim each other. If speed is not essential, then try to see which can do the length of the pool in the fewest number of strokes. This makes for powerful leg-kicks and gracefulness. I am surprized that more swimming clubs are not organized for both sexes. No sport is better enjoyed; as a health and body builder it is unsurpassed. It develops graceful lines, as our swimming Olympic mermaids show.

Why should the average person, tied to his daily task indoors, let down on his exercise when the cold weather sets in and early rising is shelved? A little will power can do wonders in keeping one in good condition all summer and winter. Twenty minutes' steady swimming in a pool three times weekly will enable a person to get in as much exercise as he could get from one hour's work in a gymnasium. All the muscles are exercised at the same time. My father, who swam the English Channel in

[193]

his day, used only one other form of exercise besides swimming, and that was walking. He walked to get himself in condition for all his long swims. For the purpose of keeping yourself fit, however, swimming alone will give you all the needed exercise. See what each stroke does for you:

The Back Stroke—Develops power in arms, thighs, and shoulders.

The Overhand—Develops thighs, knees, chest and arms.

The Breast Stroke—Develops and builds the shoulder, arm and chest muscles. The cut-through with the arms, and the backward sweep, together strengthen the shoulders. Especially good for all persons who work at desks; takes the stoop out of the shoulders.

The Side Stroke—Besides helping the shoulders and arms, this is great for the legs, as the scissors-kick, with the wide spread, develops the thighs to a remarkable extent.

The Trudgen Stroke—Being a hard stroke, this exercises the chest, arms and legs, besides forcing deep breathing.

The Crawl Stroke—Good for the same reason as the trudgen. Develops all the muscles from the waist down, besides making you breathe deeply and quickly to get buoyancy in the water.

KEEPING FIT BY SWIMMING

Not one of these strokes overdevelops the muscles of any part of the body. Swimming does not create the muscle-bound condition caused by many other exercises, but makes for long, sinewy muscles. It strengthens the muscles, makes them smooth and firm, and develops a graceful body.

A little jingle published in a magazine called *Swimming* sums up this part of the subject thus:

> Mother swims the breast stroke,
> Sister swims the crawl,
> Father swims the trudgen,
> While Brother swims 'em all;
> But Grandpa swims dog-fashion—
> It's no hifalutin name,
> But it keeps him young and healthy,
> And he gets there just the same.

FOR REDUCING ONE'S WEIGHT

How often we hear stout people say, "Oh, how I wish I were thin!" or "My weight is going up terribly—I must do something to keep my figure normal."

Now, there are two reasons why people grow

too fat. The first is laziness, and the second is —laziness! Of course, there are two classes of stout people—those who have inherited their stoutness, and those who have allowed themselves to become stout through leading too sedentary a life. For the first class, life is a constant fight to keep their weight within bounds, but for the second class the cure is only a matter of sensibly directed exercise. For both, the simplest way out is to reduce by swimming.

Swimming and swimming-strokes out of water are a great thing for reducing. I have had many people come to me regularly two or three times weekly for this purpose, and I have seen some remarkable results in the way of reduced weight. Stout people ought to swim regularly every chance they get, and see what a surprizing effect it will have on their physical condition.

Twenty to thirty minutes of swimming exercises, twice a week, will keep down the surplus weight. For this purpose I have devised special medicine-ball exercises to be used before going into the water. Clothed with heavy underwear under thick sweaters, the stout pupils use two 12-pound medicine balls, throwing them back and forth vigorously with different movements until at the end of twenty minutes I have them in a profuse perspiration. After that I roll them in a blanket and let them rest on a couch for twenty minutes, until all the perspiration has oozed out of the body. After a shower I then take them into the water for a twenty-minute exercise lesson.

Natural exercise is the great health builder and retainer, and it pays big dividends. Don't hesitate and say to yourself, "I'm sure it won't help me, I'm too fat." Nothing of the kind; easy work—easy at the start—will enable the most obstinate case to be brought under control. I find that too much water-drinking is bad for people who are trying to reduce. After sweating down one's weight, it is foolish to put it right back by excessive water-drinking.

Many stout people try to reduce by home methods. These are good if kept up, but I have noticed that they seldom are kept up long enough to do any good. Some morning when you do not feel quite up to the mark, you cut out the exercise. Soon the same thing happens again, and without realizing it the would-be weight-reducer takes the easy way and discontinues exercising. Now, with regular appointments my pupils are not allowed to discontinue their work without a real cause; if they don't show up, I 'phone them and generally shame them into continuing. They get their reward in the new zest that they feel after a good workout.

The back-stroke movements, repeated twenty or thirty times, bring the muscles of your whole body into play and help to reduce the abdomen, as well as to remove excess fat from other portions of the body. This exercise is particularly desirable for stout people, as they can lie down while doing it and take their weight off their feet. The same thing applies to the side stroke and many others. I lay out a regular home exercise schedule of swimming strokes for my reduction-course pupils.

Just visualize yourself twenty pounds lighter after two months' work three times weekly—twenty pounds less to carry around, twenty pounds less to look at in your mirror! Think of regaining your youthful figure and dancing again without effort!

As you reduce, your swimming and wind improve. Climbing stairs means no hardship;

your whole being responds to the increasing vigor of the body, and life takes on a new aspect. You see things with increased interest. Every fall I have people coming back to me for a couple of months' work to put them in shape for the winter's hard round of social or business activities.

Some people go away to expensive resorts to reduce. This reminds me of a story. A doctor once told a husband that his wife was getting too fat and needed a change of air. "But, doctor," the husband replied, "I can't afford that. I'll tell you what I'll do—I'll get her an electric fan." As a matter of fact, you can't get your body into good shape by a change of air at an expensive resort any more than by sitting in front of an electric fan.

Regular exercise two or three times weekly in the water will do the trick. Get up a little earlier, take some deep breaths at your open bedroom window, then do your swimming exercises on the floor. If time permits, take a tepid shower. I do not believe in icy showers for stout people—the shock is too much—but a shower with the chill taken off is just about right. A good brisk rub-down with a coarse turkish towel, and you will want to hurry to the breakfast table.

For lunch I advise soup, salads, and milk puddings. I never touch meat more than once a day, often not at all. But I used to train for my races on soups, calf's-foot jelly and milk puddings. This simple diet kept me in the pink of condition. Stout people need more exercise and less food. With regular morning exercise and semi-weekly swims, the weight can be kept down.

VII

WATER-POLO

VII .

WATER-POLO

AS A PASTIME

WATER-POLO has become one of the most popular and fascinating of all water sports. It can be indulged in by very good swimmers only. It affords abundant opportunity for the exhibition of skill and endurance.

For the following account of water-polo the author is indebted to a volume from Spalding's Athletic Library, entitled "Water Polo," written by L. de B. Handley, permission to use it having kindly been granted by the publishers:

The value of an athletic game or contest is determined by four things: Its physical-culture merits; its utility; its attractiveness as a pastime, and its spectacular features.

Water-polo has few equals as a means of developing the body. The swimming in it alone would insure general and symmetrical develop-

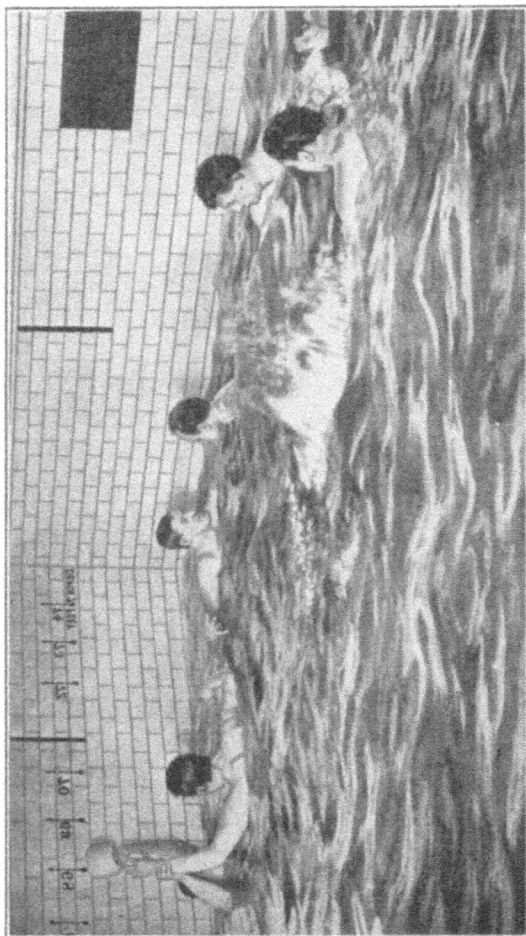

Courtesy of "Spaulding's Athletic Library."

(82) PLAYING WATER-POLO

ment, but the player wrestles besides, during a game, and every part of the body is given its proportionate share of this grueling work, developing all muscles in a uniform way.

As to its utility, it is self-evident. Swimming has come to be looked upon as a necessity, simply because it may be the means of saving life, and in this water-polo is the most practical of teachers. A player is coached on how to free himself from every kind of tackle, how to assist an exhausted team-mate and how to apply the best methods of resuscitation when any one is knocked out. It is a revelation to see an expert player handle a drowning person, and more especially a frantic one. The rescue is performed in such an easy, matter-of-fact way as to lead one to wonder at the halo of heroism that surrounds most cases of life-saving. Hardly a player but has several rescues to his credit, which he looks upon as a series of trifling services rendered to fellow mortals, and no more.

As a pastime water-polo is among the leaders. Hard and exhausting it may be, but there is an exhilaration in dashing about the pool, fighting one's way to goal, that no other game gives. And it has a feature that appeals strongly to the individual who has attained full maturity—the rarity of accidents. Bruises and knockouts one gets aplenty, but those serious injuries which mar football, hockey and lacrosse are totally unknown.

ITS EVOLUTION IN AMERICA

There is a belief that a game similar to water-polo was played by the ancients, but no actual proof of it has been found. Rules were first formulated in England in 1870, and we adopted them in America about 1890, but our present game bears absolutely no resemblance to the one then played. In the latter, points were scored by throwing an inflated rubber ball nine inches in diameter through an open goal marked by uprights and a cross-bar; and passing was the feature of the game. Americans found it unsuited. The few available tanks were so small that there was no place for action, and the outdoor season was too short to be satisfactory.

The idea was then conceived of changing

the goal into a solid surface, four feet by one in size, and of obliging the scorer to touch the ball to the goal while holding it, instead of passing it.

The innovation met ready favor, but, as may be imagined, transformed the sport. From an open passing game, water-polo became one of close formations and fierce scrimmages. These, at first, were disorderly scuffles, where weight and brute strength reigned supreme, but little by little strict rules were formulated to eliminate rough tactics, and then science became an important factor.

In 1897 a man entered the field who was destined to revolutionize the system of play.

Harold H. Reeder, of the late Knickerbocker Athletic Club, besides being a good leader and a brilliant individual player, knew how to handle men. He realized that in a growing sport new ideas would mean development, and he made it possible for the members of his squad to experiment with those they had. The system he used is worth a few words of explanation, because it was accountable for the wonderful strides made since 1897, and because every team will profit by its adoption.

SWIMMING SCIENTIFICALLY TAUGHT

Reeder, aided by Prof. Alex. Meffett, began by teaching every candidate the rudiments of the game; veterans and greenhorns alike were put through the mill. Each was schooled in the principles of swimming, diving, catching, passing, scoring, interfering, tackling and breaking, until these points had been mastered, and only then did the team practise begin. But again, no player was allowed to go in unprepared. Reeder instituted blackboard practise and saw that every one attended it. Placing before his assembled squad the possible formations, he made players selected at random explain the duties of every position in each formation. By this system he obliged every player to use his brains, and he found out the amount of water-polo intelligence that each possessed. He also imparted to each the ideas of all the others, he taught them how to fill every position and he brought to light many new plays.

The progress which the innovation was responsible for no one realized until the aggregation of yearlings from the Knickerbocker Athletic Club defeated the formidable array of champions representing the New York Athletic Club. Reeder abandoned the game two years later, but his good work lived after him, and some of his team-mates held the championship for many years by following his teachings.

HOW THE GAME IS NOW PLAYED

Water-polo as played to-day in America is rather dangerous for outdoors, and indoor pools are generally used. It is a contest between two teams of six, having as object the touching of the opponent's goal-board with an inflated rubber ball seven inches in diameter, which the referee throws into the water at the start of play.

In order to score, the ball has to be touched to the goal while in the hand of a player—except in certain cases, specified in the rules, when it must be thrown. The goals are spaces four by one foot, situated at each short end of the playing area, twelve inches above the water level. The size of the playing area is optional, tho the recognized dimensions are 60 x 40 feet or 25 x 75 feet, with a uniform depth of seven feet of water. Imaginary lines are drawn across the tank (see Fig. 83), parallel to the short ends, at four and fifteen feet from them. The first, called four-foot line, serves as protection to the goal-tenders and can not be crossed until the ball is within; the other is the foul line, and serves to mark the spot on which the forwards line up on being given a free trial. The four-foot line also marks the space in which indiscriminate tackling is allowed when the ball is within it.

Each team of six is divided into a forward line (center, right forward and left forward) whose duty it is to attack the opponent's goal; and a backfield of three (right back, left back, and goalkeeper), upon whom devolves the defense of the home goal.

At the start of play the two teams line up at their respective ends, the referee places the ball in the middle of the playing area and then blows the whistle. At this signal the twelve players dive in, the forwards to make a dash for the ball, the backs to take up their positions. The forward who first reaches the ball tosses it back to the defense men, who hold it until the line of attack is formed and then pass it back. Immediately a fierce scrimmage takes place and either a score is made or the ball changes side and a scrimmage occurs at the other end. After the score the teams line up as at start of play.

Time of play is sixteen minutes, actual, divided into two halves of eight minutes each, with an intermission of five minutes between halves. Only two substitutes are allowed, and they can be used only to replace an injured or exhausted player.

PREPARATORY WORK

No man should attempt to play water-polo who is not in the best possible physical condition. Before joining the squad, every candidate, be he a novice coming to learn the game, or a veteran resuming training, should prepare himself for the hard work in sight. I don't mean that he should be down to edge, but in good ruddy health. As a matter of fact, a man is far better off if he can start the season with eight or ten pounds of extra avoirdupois; and four or five pounds above "pink of condition" may be carried throughout the season with good results. They will prevent one's getting cold while in the water and keep one from going stale, a very easy matter in water-polo.

Preliminary exercise should be taken daily for a week or two in anticipation of starting practise. Long swims are advisable at this early date, but should be abandoned while preparing for a contest, as one sprints only in a game.

The best system to follow is a very simple one.

A few minutes in the steam-room (not more than five) or some calisthenics to warm up the blood, then a fast hundred. This done, rest until you have regained your breath. Taking the water-polo ball next, pass it to given points of the tank to secure accuracy, and sprint after it each time. Then get against the side of the tank, and placing the ball ten or twelve feet away, try to secure it with one hand on a push-off. This, done half a dozen times daily, will insure accurate passing and catching, and will obviate fumbling.

Another excellent exercise is to place the ball fifteen or twenty feet from you and then swim after it under water, trying to get it without coming to the surface. This gets you used to underwater work and accustoms you to looking. for the ball while submerged in a scrimmage.

Gymnasium work is not advisable unless one's physical condition is badly in need of building up, and even then only the lightest kind should be taken. It has too great a tendency to harden the muscles; a swimmer's should be soft and pliable.

Breathing exercises can be highly recommended; there is nothing better for the wind. It is a good plan to take these exercises while walking in the open air. By inhaling for the space of six steps, and exhaling for six, the lungs are properly worked. In cold weather breathe through the nose.

DEVELOPING NEW PLAYERS

The game of water-polo is such a strenuous one that even the best of men often tackle it with misgivings. The new player should on no account attempt to take part in a scrub game until he has thoroughly mastered the rudiments. The man who goes in against an experienced tackler, ignorant of the means of protecting himself, receives punishment so severe as to give him a completely erroneous idea of the game.

If the candidate has followed the suggestions given above he will be physically able to stand the grueling, but more is needed; he should be able to take care of himself. To teach him how, he must be taken in hand alone, and shown the various tackles and breaks.

This is best done on *terra firma;* in the water the man will be thinking of the ducking in sight and his mind will not be in receptive mood. It is also essential to make him understand each hold thoroughly before proceeding with another.

Once a man has the movements learned, he can be put in the water with a skilled player and allowed to practise on the latter, who should let him secure the holds without opposition at first, but gradually increase the resistance until he becomes proficient. If there is no one to coach, and no good player to practise against, the new men should work on each other.

Water-polo holds are a good deal a matter of individuality; each man builds up a set of his own, but one tackle and one break will serve as a foundation for all.

To learn the tackle, give your coworker the ball and let him come toward you. When he's a couple of feet off, take a good, hard stroke, lift yourself as high out of the water as you can, throw your arm around his neck, and pulling his head down until it is jammed hard against your chest, wind your legs around his body. Then you have him at your mercy, and you can proceed to take the ball away from him. This tackle should be learned by forwards and backs alike; all need it.

The best break known is the following: We will suppose that you carry the ball in the right hand. On approaching your opponent, throw your left shoulder forward, presenting a three-quarter view. To tackle you effectively he must use his right arm, as you could easily repel a left-handed one in your position. As soon as his right arm goes up, place your left hand squarely under his armpit and let yourself sink, twisting around, face toward him, as you pass under, and as soon as you are on your back force his body over you. Then plant both feet on him and shove off. In most cases, if you succeed, you will find yourself between your opponent and his goal, where all you have to do is to touch the board for a score.

To use the legs at every possible chance should be a principle of the player. Once an opponent is caught in a good leg-hold he is rendered helpless. Incidentally, the wise player ceases struggling when he recognizes that he is caught beyond freeing. It is an excellent rule also to avoid being tackled uselessly; if a body encounter is liable to let you out best, or will help your side, go into it heart and soul, just as hard as you know how, but never make a senseless sacrifice.

Passing and catching are all-important factors in water-polo and should be practised constantly. In passing it is well to bear in mind that the object in view is to give the ball securely to one's team-mate. Pass high and carefully; a low throw may be intercepted and a hard one fumbled. Especially in close quarters high passing is essential.

To cover one's opponent when the other side has the ball and get away from him when one's own has it, should be the religion of every player. In covering him, always stay back of him, where you can watch him, and tackle him just in the nick of time if the ball is passed to him.

Many new men have an idea that one knows intuitively how to score, but it is not so. The various ways must be learned. One only does in a game what one has become used to in practise, for there is little time or chance to think in the excitement of a keen contest, and it is those things which have been ground into one by dint of repetition that stand by one. To get used to scoring, place yourself three or four yards from goal and then sink yourself, or let some one else put you under, and try to come up and hit the board with eyes closed; you will soon find what a difference practise makes. You must also learn how to hurdle by letting some one tread water between you and goal and score by placing your free hand on his shoulder and lifting yourself over.

A short course of this kind, and you will be ready to line up.

A FEW POINTS

On entering the tank for an important game, every player should forget his individuality and submit passively to the orders of the captain. There must be only one head for a team to succeed, and an order should be executed without hesitation and without questioning; right or wrong, the best results come through blind obedience. The man giving the orders often sees an opening that the other does not.

Let no personal difference affect your game; play to win, not to pay off an old score. It is the goals made, not the men disabled, that give one victory, and victory is what every player should seek.

To the forward, discrimination is a valuable asset. When caught in a tackle so far away from goal that getting free will not help you pass the ball at once, don't allow your opponent to punish you. But if you are nailed within easy reach of goal, fight as long as there is breath of life in you. Never mind how hopeless the task may seem, a team-mate may come to the rescue at any moment, and then you'll score.

The forward should always play the ball in preference to the man and keep free as much as possible. And above all—play fast and hard.

WATER-POLO RULES
Copyright, 1926, by National Collegiate Athletic Association.

RULE I. PLAYING AREA

SECTION 1. The length of the playing area shall be not greater than 75 feet nor less than 60 feet. The width of the playing area shall be not greater than 40 feet nor less than 20 feet. All pools shall conform as nearly as possible to these dimensions.

Note.—When pools have a shallow end it is advisable to shorten the playing area by placing a spar with goal attached across the pool so as to insure a playing area 6 feet deep.

SEC. 2. The following lines on each side of the playing area shall be plainly marked:

1. Center line—equidistant from ends.
2. Four-foot lines—4 feet from ends.
3. Fifteen-foot lines—15 feet from ends.
4. Twenty-foot lines—20 feet from ends.

SEC. 3. The two 20-foot areas at the ends of the pool shall be called the *goal zones*.

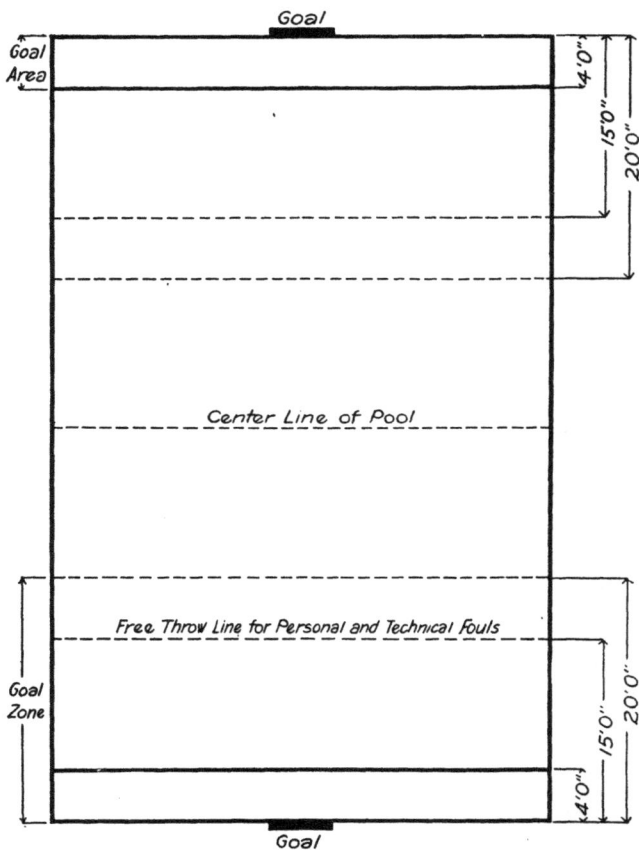

Goal

Goal Area

4'0"

15'0"

20'0"

Center Line of Pool

Free Throw Line for Personal and Technical Fouls

Goal Zone

20'0"

15'0"

4'0"

Goal

(83) WATER-POLO FIELD OF PLAY

WATER-POLO

RULE II. THE GOALS

SECTION 1. The goals shall be boards 4 feet in length and 18 inches in height and marked in large letters with the word *goal*.

SEC. 2. They shall be located at the ends of the playing area 12 inches above the water level and equidistant from the sides.

RULE III. THE BALL

SECTION 1. The ball shall be the regulation white rubber water-polo ball, not less than 7 nor more than 8 inches in diameter.

SEC. 2. It should be inflated seven-eighths full and free from oil, grease or other objectionable substance so that a good grip may be had on it with one hand, and it shall be inspected by the referee before putting it into play to see that the inflation is as described.

SEC. 3. The home team shall supply an official ball.

RULE IV. PLAYERS AND SUBSTITUTES

SECTION 1. The team shall consist of six players in the following positions: Center, Right Forward, Left Forward, Right Back, Left Back, and Goal-keeper.

SEC. 2. The captains must be playing members of their teams. All protests, all demands for cessation of play for any purpose whatsoever, and no-

[221]

tices of substitution of players must be made to the referee by the captains.

SEC. 3. A player may be substituted for another at any time, provided that his side has possession of the ball, or at any time at the discretion of the referee. Before entering the water the new player must report to, and be recognized by, the referee.

SEC. 4. Only two men may be substituted in any one championship game unless it is otherwise agreed by both captains before the start of the game. A player who has been removed during the game for other reasons than disqualification may be returned during the subsequent period.

RULE V. OFFICIALS

SECTION 1. There shall be the following officials:

Referee.
Two Timekeepers.
Two Goal Umpires.
One Scorer.

SEC. 2. The referee must be selected and mutually agreed upon by the official representatives of both teams. He shall be supplied with a whistle and pistol for signaling.

Note.—It is advisable for each league to have an approved list of officials from which to choose.

SEC. 3. The umpires shall call attention to any

fouls, shall give evidence on the scoring of goals if called upon, but may not stop the game.

SEC. 4. The timekeepers shall be chosen by mutual agreement of the two captains. They shall be supplied with stop-watches and whistles and shall keep time on the game.

SEC. 5. The referee shall have absolute supervision of the game, shall have the power to reverse any decision of an umpire, and shall call fouls when necessary.

SEC. 6. In case of a foul the referee shall indicate the offender and announce the nature of the foul, so that the scorer, offender, and spectators can hear him.

RULE VI. THE GAME

SECTION 1. The game shall consist of two periods, or halves, of eight minutes each, with an intermission of five minutes.

SEC. 2. In the case of a tie at the end of the second period, the teams shall rest five minutes and then play for another period of three minutes, or as many such periods as may be necessary to break the tie.

SEC. 3. A captain, provided his team is in possession of the ball, may call time out without penalty up to two minutes for any purpose, but not more than twice in one period. On resumption of play the teams shall line up at their respective ends, with the ball in possession of the goalkeeper of the team that called time out. Time occupied by disputes, repairing of suits, replacing of men, lining up for new start, and free throws from fouls, shall not be counted as time of play.

SEC. 4. When for any reason the referee wishes to call time or stop play during any period, he shall sound the whistle or pistol. This signal shall immediately render the ball dead, and the ball so stopped shall not again be put into play except by the referee, who shall give it to the goalkeeper of the team having it last, both teams lining up at their respective ends.

SEC. 5. Time shall be taken out whenever the ball goes out of bounds, time out to begin when the referee's whistle or pistol sounds calling the ball out of bounds, and time in again shall begin when the referee's whistle or pistol sounds calling the ball in play.

SEC. 6. The start at the beginning of each period shall be made by both teams lining up at their respective ends of the pool, the visitors being given choice at beginning of first period. The ball shall be placed in the center of the playing area by the referee and held there with a pole fitted with a ring, start for the ball being made only at the sound of the whistle or pistol. In case of a false start, teams shall line up as before. Three consecutive false starts by one of the teams shall constitute a technical

WATER-POLO

foul. Teams shall change ends at half time and at the beginning of each extra period.

RULE VII. DEFINITION OF THE TERMS

SECTION 1. The ball shall be considered in play until it either leaves the playing area or the referee signals with whistle or pistol.

SEC. 2. To score a touch goal the ball must be touched to the goal while in the possession of a player on the attacking side. To score a thrown goal, the ball must strike the goal board after being thrown by a member of the attacking team from outside the 15-foot line. If the ball is in the air when time is called and a goal is scored, the goal shall count.

SEC. 3. After a touch goal or a thrown goal has been scored, the teams shall line up at their respective ends of the playing area and the ball shall be given to the goalkeeper of the side scored upon, and at the signal by whistle of the referee all the men of both teams must enter the water immediately from their respective ends of the pool under penalty of a technical foul, and in ten seconds the goalkeeper holding the ball must pass or carry it out of his goal zone. When the ball is in a team's own zone a player on that team may retain possession of it not longer than ten seconds or until the umpire or referee signals by word, at which signal the ball must pass out of that goal zone or be forfeited to the goalkeeper of the opposing team. After a free throw, whether successful or not, the ball shall be given to the goalkeeper of the team fouled against and the ball shall be put in play in the same manner as after a touch or thrown goal.

SEC. 4. If a team causes the ball to go out of the playing area, it shall be given to the goalkeeper of the opposing team within his own 4-foot line; and the players of the team causing the ball to go out shall not be allowed within the 15-foot line until the whistle or pistol is sounded. No player shall leave the water when the ball goes out of bounds.

SEC. 5. The ball shall be kept on or as near the surface as possible and shall not be intentionally carried under the water. If, however, a player with the ball has been forced under by an opponent, he may carry the ball as far as eight feet under water. The ball shall not be carried under water a greater distance than this under any circumstances. No goal shall be counted if scored on an under water pass,

No player shall hold on to the side or end of the pool except for the purpose of resting and shall take no part in the play while resting.

SEC. 6. No player, except three backs of the defending side, shall be allowed inside the 4-foot line until the ball is within it. When the ball is within this line no player inside this section will be

WATER-POLO

allowed artificial support other than the bottom of the playing area.

SEC. 7. No player shall tackle an opponent unless said opponent has possession of the ball or is within four feet of the ball. EXCEPTION.—When ball is within the 4-foot section tackling may be allowed anywhere within this section. At other times a player in covering an opponent may block him, but shall not lay hands on him or hold him with his legs.

RULE VIII. FOULS

SECTION 1. Fouls are divided into three groups: personal, technical, and disqualifying.

SEC. 2. The penalty for a personal foul shall be two free throws at an unguarded goal from the 15-foot mark; each throw if successful will count one point. Personal fouls are enumerated as follows:

a. Tackling player who is not within 4 feet of ball.

b. Delaying the game after receiving notification to play by the referee.

c. Kicking intentionally or striking an opponent.

d. Holding under water for more than ten seconds any player who is within 4 feet of the ball. EXCEPTION.—A player who has possession of the ball may be held under ten seconds or as long thereafter as he retains possession of the ball.

SWIMMING SCIENTIFICALLY TAUGHT

e. Unnecessary rough work.

f. Tackling player after goal has been scored or after game has been stopped for any reason by referee.

g. Use of abusive language to players or officials.

h. Player other than captain questioning any decision of officials.

i. Violation of Rule VII, Sec. 7, regarding blocking.

j. Tackling a player by the costume.

SEC. 3. The penalty for a technical foul shall be a free throw at an unguarded goal from the 15-foot mark, which if successful will count one point. Technical fouls are as follows:

a. Crossing 4-foot line ahead of ball. (If player corrects this mistake at once, provided the mistake has in no way affected the play, no foul shall be called.)

b. Holding on side or end of pool while engaged in scrimmage or while in possession of the ball.

c. Substitute failing to report to referee.

d. Swimming under water more than 8 feet with the ball.

e. Three false starts on line-up.

f. Four players inside their own 4-foot line when ball is not in goal section. EXCEPTION.—If the defending side fouls after the ball is within 4-foot line and a goal is scored the foul shall not count. If, however, the goal is not scored, the foul shall count and a free throw given to the offended side.

g. Failure to enter water according to Rule VII, Sec. 3.

h. Holding ball under water unless *tackled* by opponent.

i. Violation of Rule VII, Sec. 6, regarding artificial support.

j. Going under water with the ball before being tackled.

Sec. 4. A player may be suspended for the period or disqualified for the game by the referee for unnecessary roughness or for unbecoming conduct and his team charged with a personal foul. A substitute shall be allowed for a suspended player, but the suspended player may return to the game at the beginning of the subsequent period. When a player is disqualified a substitute may take his place immediately.

Sec. 5. Any player having oil, grease, or other objectionable substance on his body or suit shall be disqualified.

Sec. 6. If the attacking side fouls and before the foul is called a goal is scored by them, the loss of the goal shall be the only penalty, and the ball shall be put in play in the center of the pool as at the beginning of the game.

RULE IX. SCORING

Section 1. Goal values:
A touch goal will equal 5 points.

A thrown goal will equal 3 points.

A goal thrown by free throw after foul will equal 1 point.

Sec. 2. The team scoring the largest number of points shall be declared the winner.

Sec. 3. It is recommended that the home team provide a scoreboard of such dimensions and so placed as to enable players and spectators to follow the game more easily.

VIII

WHAT TO DO IN EMERGENCIES

VIII

WHAT TO DO IN EMERGENCIES

CRAMPS

To BE suddenly seized with cramps is a thing likely to happen to most expert swimmers. Cramp is due to various causes—staying too long in the water and getting chilled, going in after a heavy meal, stiffening the legs too much, and varicose veins. Preventive: Never remain in the water after feeling chilled; always swim around and exercise yourself. For persons not in training, twenty minutes is long enough to remain in the water. Always turn over on the back when getting a cramp, and float, at the same time working toward the shore with the hands, and don't lose your presence of mind.

Don't attempt to rescue a person from drowning unless you are a good swimmer yourself; remember that a drowning person is generally insane for the time being, and is liable to

drag you to your death unless you are capable
of swimming with a heavy load.

METHODS OF RESCUE

When one accidentally falls overboard, or
is compelled to leap into deep water, the first
essential is to keep one's presence of mind. Do
not feel alarmed if your head should go under
once or twice—you are bound to come to the
surface, and will be able to sustain yourself for
a considerable time, even if you are not a swimmer, if you will but keep your hands under
water. The reason so many people drown is
because directly they come to the surface they
raise their hands above their heads and shout
for help. This is fatal. The moment the hands
are raised out of the water the body will sink
below the surface.

Another thing to remember is to keep the
mouth closed until the body attains the floating position; then try to breathe naturally
through the mouth and help propel yourself
with your hands. Should you be able to swim,
try to take off your outer clothing, as this,

when water-soaked, tends to drag the body down, besides retarding one's movements.

To risk one's life in order to save a fellow being from drowning is one of the most heroic acts that one may be called upon to perform, yet how many of us have the presence of mind and courage to act in such an emergency? To rescue a person from drowning is no child's play, even for the best swimmers; it requires pluck, nerve, and stamina. Of course, I allude to rescues which take place some distance from shore. Many a daring swimmer has been clutched and dragged down to death simply because he did not know the safest way to approach a drowning person.

Of the many different ways of saving life, the safest and best method is to swim as near the person as possible, then dive under and come up behind him; otherwise he is liable to grab you around the neck with a death clutch, from which it is extremely difficult to escape. When swimming up behind the person, grab his biceps and force him on his back (Fig. 84); the more he struggles the more he helps himself to keep afloat.

To prevent being clutched by a drowning person the following rules should be carefully studied. Every action, however, must be prompt and decisive, otherwise this method will be of no avail.

(84) BEST POSITION, AS A RULE, IN SAVING LIFE

1. If grasped by the wrists, turn both arms simultaneously against the drowning person, thumbs outward, and attempt to bring your arms at right angles to your own body. This will dislocate the thumbs of the drowning person and he must let go his hold.

[236]

2. If clutched around the neck, immediately take a deep breath, lean well over your opponent, place the left hand in the small part of his back and draw your right arm in an upward direction until in line with his shoulder, and pass it at once over his arm. Then with the thumb and forefinger catch his nose and pinch the nostrils close, at the same time place the palm of your hand on his chin and push firmly outward. This will cause him to open his mouth for breathing purposes, and he, being under you, will swallow water. Choking ensues, and not only is the rescuer freed, but the other is left so helpless as to be completely under control.

3. If clutched around the body and arms, take a deep breath, lean well over your opponent and throw the right arm in an upward direction at right angles to the body, or draw it up between your body and that of your opponent. Then with the thumb and forefinger catch the nose and pinch the nostrils close, and at the same time place the palm of the hand on the chin and bring the right knee as high as possible up between the two bodies, placing it, if possible, against the lower part of your oppo-

nent's chest; then, by means of a strong and somewhat sudden push, stretch your arms and legs out straight, at the same time throwing the whole weight of the body backward. The sudden motion will press the air out of the other's lungs, as well as push him off, no matter how tightly he may be holding. He may then be seized from behind and rescued in the manner indicated in Fig. 84.

Should the drowning person act sensibly and not try to grab his rescuer, he can be brought in by placing his hands on his rescuer's shoulders and kicking out his legs behind him while the rescuer swims in toward shore. The saved person in this case trails along on his back beneath the rescuer, his mouth above water, his arms and hands barely submerged; he must continue in sufficient possession of his wits, however, to keep his arms straightened out enough to enable the rescuer's breast strokes to propel him to safety in this easy position. This is one of the best ways of carrying a tired swimmer to safety if he has become exhausted and is still in full possession of his reasoning powers.

Another method is to pull the person on his

back by holding him under the right armpit with your right hand and using the left hand and legs to swim with. (Fig. 85.) Should the rescue be close to shore, swim behind the person and help by pushing him in toward shallow water. Should the drowning person have

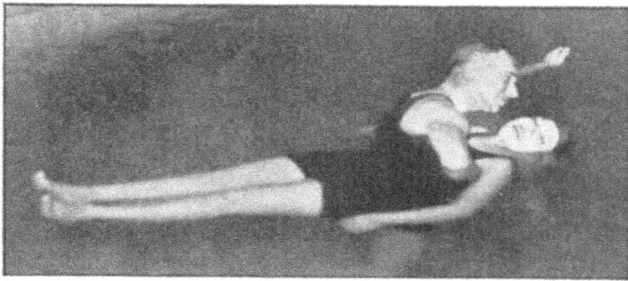

(85) PROPER POSITION WHEN DROWNING PERSON DOES NOT STRUGGLE

sunk, watch when the air-bubbles rise to the surface. At once dive down perpendicularly to the bottom when the air-bubbles show, seize the drowning person and bring him to the surface by pushing off from the bottom and using your legs to send you upward to the surface. Before trying to rescue any one, get rid of as much clothing as possible, if time will permit.

[239]

RESUSCITATION AFTER RESCUE

After bringing a drowning person ashore your work is only half done; the next thing is to restore him to consciousness should he be unconscious. There are several methods for resuscitating the apparently drowned. The method adopted by the Royal Humane Society of England is one of the simplest. It is as follows:

Begin treatment in the open air as soon as you have brought the unfortunate ashore. Meanwhile send for medical assistance, blankets, and dry clothing. Expose the patient's throat and chest to the wind, except in very severe weather. Remove all tight clothing from neck and chest. Take off suspenders.

The points to be aimed at are: First and immediately the restoration of breathing, and, secondly, after breathing is restored, the promotion of warmth and circulation. The efforts to restore breathing must be commenced immediately and energetically (for method to be employed see next section), and persevered in for one or two hours, or until a medical man has pronounced life extinct.

Efforts to promote warmth and circulation beyond removing the wet clothes and drying the skin must not be made until the first appearance of natural breathing, for if circulation of the blood be induced before breathing has recommenced the patient's life will be endangered.

ARTIFICIAL RESPIRATION

The Prone Pressure (Schaefer) method of resuscitating persons who are apparently drowned or asphyxiated is summarized by the American National Red Cross as follows:

When the patient is removed from the water, gas, smoke, or electric contact, get to work at once with your own hands. If possible, send for a physician.

Lay the patient on his stomach. Extend one arm directly over head. Bend the other arm at elbow, and rest patient's cheek on hand, to keep the nose and mouth off the ground and free for breathing.

Kneel facing forward, and straddling patient's legs just above the knees. Place palms of hands on

[241]

each side of back, just above belt line, and about
four inches apart, thumbs and fingers together, the
little fingers over and following the line of the lowest
ribs, and the tips of fingers just out of sight.
(Fig. 86.)

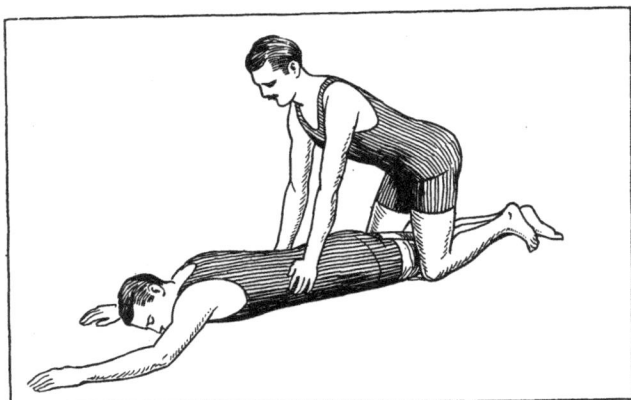

(86) ARTIFICIAL BREATHING—FORWARD MOVEMENT WITH
STRAIGHT-ARM PRESSURE

With arms straight, lean gradually forward,
pressing downward and forward and counting
slowly, one, two, three. Snap your hands sideways,
off patient's back. Swing your body back, counting
slowly, four, five. (Fig. 87.) Rest. Straighten
arms and repeat pressure.

Three movements, straight arm pressure (shoulder behind hands so that pressure is exerted for-

ward), quick release, and swing back. To assist in timing these movements (about 12 per minute) repeat during period of pressure: "Out goes the bad air." Snap off your hands and repeat during period of release: "In comes the good." Keep up work

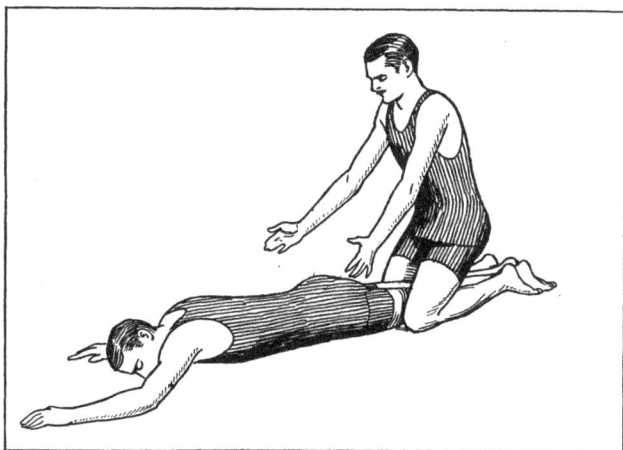

(87) ARTIFICIAL BREATHING—BACKWARD SWING WITH QUICK RELEASE

steadily until breathing begins and continues naturally. Unless a physician takes charge, remove patient well covered on a stretcher to a hospital or to his home.

This same Prone Pressure method—the best

[243]

that science has discovered—is described more in detail by the Red Cross in these words:

In application of artificial respiration, save the seconds and you have a better chance of saving the life. Don't waste time carrying victim to a quiet spot. Work where he is taken from the water. Waste no time trying to get the harmless water out of the stomach. Turn subject face down and go to work instantly.

Often inexperienced or excited persons attempt to administer artificial respiration when there is no need for such treatment. It is required only when the victim is unable to breathe. If victim is brought from water unconscious, but breathing, he requires treatment for fainting or shock; that is, raising the feet, leaving the head low; applying stimulants such as aromatic spirits near nose; rubbing limbs and body toward heart to stimulate circulation.

The Prone Pressure method is a most effective imitation of the natural process of breathing, because it utilizes the diaphragm and the muscular elasticity of the chest to produce a natural inhalation of air. It is more effective than any other known manual method, because of the face-downward position of the patient, in which his tongue drops forward of its own accord, eliminating the necessity for holding it. Only one operator is necessary. The method does not require great physical exertion on the part of the operator, permitting him to continue for some time without rest.

Lay the victim face downward on flat surface or with head slightly downhill. Turn his head to one side, extend both arms up beyond head, and place one hand under face to protect his open mouth and nose from dirt. Kneel (straddling one or both knees) facing subject's head.

To find point of pressure, scrape the lower edge of hands down the ribs from the shoulders, until they stop in the soft place between the hip joint and the lowest ribs. Start pressure with hands encircling lower ribs. The wrists are about four inches apart, one on each side of backbone, the thumbs folded against the fingers to form a pressure pad. If hands are in the correct position, the little finger of each hand is over and following the line of the lowest rib.

Move weight of your body slowly downward and forward for about three seconds—don't slide. Keep arms straight. The shoulders should be behind the hands, so that pressure exerted is forward. Then snap the hands off, allowing ribs to expand quickly, filling lungs with air. Swing body slowly backward to upright position, thus relaxing the muscles of the back.

At the end of two seconds again place hands in position and apply pressure. This timing (three seconds pressure and two seconds release) uses five seconds for one complete respiration, assuring twelve respirations per minute. This is fast enough and will allow the operator to continue for some time without exhaustion.

As soon as helpers arrive, put them to work. Send for a doctor, for warm bottles or bricks, and for tea or coffee for stimulant. When you need rest, let one of your workers take your place. One may clean patient's mouth, stimulating reflexes by moving tongue back and forth. Patient's clothing may be loosened, and his body and limbs rubbed toward the heart to stimulate circulation. Covering and heated articles may be applied. (Be careful to avoid burning patient.)

Don't give up!—Persons who have been under water as long as thirty minutes have been resuscitated by this simple method. There is no certain sign by which the layman can determine that it is too late for artificial respiration. If no results are seen, the subject should not be abandoned until at least two hours' effort has been made to revive him.

When subject begins to breathe and can swallow, give a teaspoonful of aromatic spirits of ammonia in half a glass of water. Hot water, tea or coffee may be used as a stimulant if aromatic spirits of ammonia is not available. Should the patient be inclined to vomit (which is a favorable sign), turn him on his right side to facilitate it. Don't allow patient to walk or otherwise exert himself. After such an experience, a person requires medical attention and should be put to bed.

WHAT TO DO IN EMERGENCIES

In all cases of prolonged immersion in cold water, when the breathing continues, a warm bath should be employed to restore the temperature.

www.ingramcontent.com/pod-product-compliance
Lightning Source LLC
Chambersburg PA
CBHW030921090426
42737CB00007B/274